IT WAS Meant to Be

SYLVIA BAIZE

TSPA THE SELF PUBLISHING AGENCY INC

Sylvia Baize

It Was Meant To Be

TSPA The Self Publishing Agency Inc.

First Edition

Print ISBN 978-1-954233-00-3

Cover & Book Design | Kristy Hill

Editor | Elise Volkman

Publishing Support | TSPA The Self Publishing Agency Inc.

I dedicate this book to the Painter of life.

And to my soulmate, Pat, and our amazing children, Lissandra, Marcio, Rafael, Alex, Lilie, and Ariana. You made the colors of this story so exquisitely beautiful. Without you, it would be no story at all.

I praise you because I am fearfully and wonderfully made; your works are wonderful, I know that full well. My frame was not hidden from you when I was made in the secret place, when I was woven together in the depths of the earth. Your eyes saw my unformed body; all the days ordained for me were written in your book before one of them came to be. How precious to me are your thoughts, God! How vast is the sum of them! Were I to count them, they would outnumber the grains of sand...

~Psalms 139:14-18a NIV

FOREWORD

Sylvia writes with openness, sincerity, and humor; but above all, her story is full of love and compassion. I am in an extremely fortunate position to know Sylvia, her lovely husband Pat, and their children.

This story depicts the strength of union and the power of God as Sylvia and Pat face, and overcome, challenge after challenge. Each chapter leaves the reader anxious to quickly begin reading the next, which is quite a rarity in the modern-day age!

The children are incredibly special, too. Special in that they are brave, courageous, and born survivors. Each one beautiful in their own unique way but all have one thing that connects them: the love of parents whose hearts are warmer than a mid-summer's afternoon and who will always be there for them and who will always overcome any obstacle put in their way.

Great book written by a great person. Thank you for the inspiration.

— Dr Daniel Nightingale, Clinical Dementia Specialist & Clinical Hypno-Psychotherapist, Fellow of the Royal Society of Medicine.

PROLOGUE

The room we waited in was small. It was pretty much a toy room meant for children to have something to do while they waited with their excited parents-to-be to be called into the courtroom. They had sent someone down to escort us up to the third floor. On the way up, people had looked our way and said, "Must be an adoption!" They could tell every time; everyone dresses their best for adoptions! We just wondered if they could tell how very special ours was. Waiting for a baby for three years and going through some pretty turbulent waters during that time had a way of making our adoption day feel very, very special.

There were two things that kept it from being completely perfect, but they were only small flies in the ointment. Every ointment must have one at least. Not much could dampen our joy that day!

Our first fly was that Oma (Frances) and Opa (Nathan) couldn't be with us for this special day. Oma and Opa had been our soon-to-be son's foster parents for the first seven months of his life. A few months after Alex had been transistioned from their home to ours, they took off for Tanzania to live a "simpler life." We couldn't blame them, but we sure did miss them.

The next fly was that Alex was having some headaches, so he wasn't feeling the best. He obliged us by being alert and happy, even though there were two social workers fighting over him and passing him back and forth like five year olds fighting over a doll. He was a hefty sixteen month old and not exactly easy to hold. That did not slow them down at all! The noise they made should have had the security guard onto us, but no such luck. They fought without disturbance. At that moment it was probably best that Oma wasn't there, otherwise there would have been three in the fight and I hadn't brought earplugs.

The third fly was that the social worker from our agency had not been able to join us. He had been right there for us for so much of our adoption journey, it seemed a bit incomplete without him there to enjoy the grand finale.

The hearing was in a tall building in downtown San Jose. It was me and my husband Pat, our children, Lissandra, Marcio, and Rafael, Alex's first social worker (one of the fighters), his replacement social worker (the other fighter), the adoption social worker (a peaceable one, at least), Smitty and Bridget (Oma's two children), and Oma's good friend Patti.

The adoption social worker had arranged for the adoption to be on the 12th of May so we could have this really awesome judge who was good at keeping it down to earth and relaxed. We were glad she had!

When we were called into the judge's quarters we walked past the Sheriff who stood just inside the door, then past a bookshelf full of stuffed animals. We sat down by a big u-shaped desk. The judge walked in to meet us and personally greeted each person in the room. When she brought out all the paperwork to be signed, she also brought a basket of party favors and had the children choose as many as they wanted. It was like a birthday party for them.

Once she started the paperwork, we gave her Alex's new name. He would no longer be Dylan Jonathan Doe. He would be our own Alex Joseph Baize from then on. She had a little ceremony where she read to us a declaration of our commitment to loving and caring for Alex and then had us sign it. Things got a little emotional at that point. We heard the two "fighters" standing behind us sniffling. Then one gave a silly little laugh and said she had never cried at an adoption before. The other one giggled and said she hadn't either. The judge got out the kleenex box and there was laughing and blowing noses for a bit, but we soon dried our tears. I didn't get to see if the sheriff had tears or not, but he said it was his first time witnessing an adoption and he was so touched that he was going to pursue his dream of adopting. He had not known it could be so beautiful. Neither had we.

When all the signing was done, the judge told the children to each pick a stuffed animal to add to their stash. Alex picked a stuffed chicken and we left loaded with gifts. But the greatest gift was the way she made it all so special. It seemed like a ray of God's love shone down on us in that room. We felt so blessed to have some of the most special people in Alex's life there to share our joy!

We began our goodbyes and soon all that was left were the three social workers to accompany us down. The fighting over Alex began again before we even left the judge's quarters. Our family and the social workers hadn't seen each other in a while, so we tried to catch up between Alex being smothered and tossed from one to another. We could hardly part ways, knowing it might be the last time we ever saw each other. Finally, someone said something about appointments to go to, so we said our reluctant goodbyes and left. Our little family went for lunch to our favorite taco place where Frances used to take us to when we would go there to see Alex. It was a lovely celebration!

This was the close of a long, grueling, but beautiful chapter in our lives. Needless to say, it also began the next adventure.

CHAPTER 1

I was born and raised in beautiful Brazil. My parents, Charles and Faith Becker, moved from Kansas to Brazil along with several other Holdeman Mennonite families around the 1970s where they pioneered and tamed the wild land near Rio Verde in the state of Goias. I had two biological siblings (Carlos and Yolanda) and three adopted siblings (Denise, Sandy, and Lucas) to welcome me into the world. My sister, Yolanda, I don't remember. I was one and a half when, at age nine, she was struck and killed by lightning while playing under a tree at school. My mom was sick during my early years so my oldest sister, Denise, took care of me and we became very close. When I was four, Denise got married. I missed having her by me everyday, but loved when I could go to her house for sleepovers and even more when it was for a whole week.

When Sandy turned eighteen, she left home and got married. She also left the Mennonite church. Because of this, we were not allowed to see her for a long time. It was heartbreaking for me as a little girl and I did not understand it.

Lucas was closest to me in age, but was eight years older than me. He was the one I rode horses with, played with, milked cows with, and heard fantastic tales from. He died a tragic death in his early forties. I was heartbroken as I had not seen him in nearly twenty years and would never see him again on this earth.

When I was seven years old, Otávio entered our lives at fourteen days old when my parents adopted him. To me he was a living doll! My mom trusted me a lot and would let me carry him around and pretend he was my doll for hours at a time. I'm sure my bossy nature had a great deal to do with his upbringing. My mom called me "the sergeant" because I certainly loved to boss that little brother around. Otávio, in turn, had a mind of his own. A clash of wills often ensued between us.

Though these are my siblings, I have many brothers and sisters that aren't recorded on paper. We had someone living with us off and on all my growing up years. My mom was known by many people as "*Mãezona*," meaning big mom and my dad was "*Paizão*"(big dad).

My dad owned a small feed store in town and two of his employees became a big part of our lives. My parents welcomed my best friend, Sherilyn, and enjoyed her coming in and out of our home. Many a slumber party we had out under the stars, dreaming about and planning our futures (we were never going to get married, but would use our time wisely and invent a clothes folding machine and have an orphanage). We were inseperable and drove many a more sober minded individual half crazy with our unstoppable zest for life and crazy humor.

In my early teens, Tamara walked into my life and became like a sister to me and Sherilyn. She was fifteen and lived in Canada. She was visiting family in Brazil. We were a threesome and the earth quaked with our laughter and escapades. We laughed so much in those few months she was visiting that we should have never been sick a day in our lives – with laughter's claim to being the cure of all ills.

When I was seventeen, Janete age nineteen, came to stay with us for two weeks. She was a cousin to my oldest adopted siblings. When my mom told me she was coming, I was teaching school and we had a foster girl that was mostly my responsibility. I felt like my plate was full enough. But come she did, whether I thought it ideal or not, and as fate would have it we became instant sisters. She became an unexpected blessing, as she loved children and was able to take over the responsibility of keeping our foster girl, SueEllen, company while I was teaching. Her two weeks stretched out to indefinite and I was glad she stayed, although some days I felt like I was working with a wild, overgrown child. She was ever and always trying to catch up on some childhood playing she claimed she'd missed. Me, I'd had my childhood. I was ready to be a grown up so a lot of times we didn't agree on the day's activities. I chose to read a book (often with a squirt bottle of window cleaner beside me to get her good if she came around to pester me and disturb my reading) while she played in the rain with the little kids. I chose to clean house while she dissected frogs.

One thing we did agree on was rough-housing. We had fun to no end. Well, until it got under my dad's skin and the game got shut down. One day he said we had gone past the limits, which struck us funny and so we had to take our hilarity to our room. It's a wonder we didn't get booted out of the house.

The house got quieter when some missionaries in southern Brazil needed assistance with their Portuguese and Janete went to teach them. While she was there, my parents, my little brother, my best friend Sherilyn, and myself drove fourteen hours to see her. We stayed in a u-shaped motel and we got the third floor to ourselves. My parents' room was at one tip of the "u" and us girls' room was at the other tip. The halls had tile floors and they echoed. My poor parents could hear us clear in their room. I have to say, it was impossible to have a quiet conversation with Sherilyn. Whatever she said was done in clear, very audible tones, especially if she got excited. The motel people never came and told us to quiet it down so all our noise must have stayed on our floor or the other guests must have all fled.

One night, one of the girls (likely Sherilyn, she was gifted with accidentism) opened the fridge and a glass bottle fell out and broke when it hit the floor. I don't remember what was so funny, but her and Janete got the giggles. I decided to go shower about the time they called down to the service desk requesting a maid to come clean it up. The girls had picked up the biggest pieces of glass and put them in the bathroom trash, but the floor needed mopping.

I was showering and the girls decided to make me miserable by knocking on the door and telling me to get out quick, but I couldn't for the life of me get out of them why. Janete could be a regular pain so I finally just ignored her and showered on. She could imitate people very well, including voice inflections, so I was sure she was up to no good. Then the knocking became more persistent and I was done with their wolf cries. I turned off the shower and I could hear a sweet voice saying, “It's Rita, my love.” I just knew Janete was at it again. I sassed her back and told her to leave me alone. Then I heard Janete and Sherilyn laughing hysterically. Choking with laughter, Janete managed to tell me that indeed, the maid, Rita, needed to see the glass in the trash to confirm that it was the one from the fridge.

Now, that sounded as crazy as anything they'd come up with yet. I refused to open the door or believe that the maid was actually there. When I finally opened the door, there stood the maid with the sweet voice. She was able to get the trash can inspected, clean the mess, and leave all in one piece, poor girl, but it's a wonder. Then began the fuss about whose fault it was the maid was kept waiting at the bathroom door so long. For years after that, all one of us girls had to say was, "It's Rita, my love" and we would burst into peals of laughter.

Soon after Janete returned from her little mission, she married a quiet boy I went to school with. Poor Edinei. Little did he know how not-quiet his days would be from then on, but my life sure was quieter!

I got a bit side tracked with my fond recollections, but now it's time to introduce Pat's family. His parents are Norman and Judy Baize and his two oldest siblings are Jill and Phil. Next came Patrick, and then Bethany. Pat was born in Arizona where he grew up with Mexican children for playmates and they always seemed to have someone coming and going at their place, including foster children.

They moved to California when Pat was twelve, where he lived until he moved to South Dakota at age twenty-four. He lived with his sister, Jill, and her husband, Dave. He loved the wide open plains but found it harder to get good lasting jobs. He worked for farmers and worked for his uncle laying brick for a while. Being a people person, he enjoyed it when his work allowed him to interact with others. He missed the lightheartedness of the Mexican culture and the mountains lining the horizons of California and Arizona.

When I met Pat the first time, he was still living in California, so I got to meet all of his family but

Jill. Pat and I lived in South Dakota after we got married and that's when I got to know Jill and Dave.

I could not have asked for a funner family to marry into. They definitely made leaving my beloved Brazil a tad less painful!

CHAPTER 2

I was fifteen when my parents and I agreed to foster children for the Koehn family from Kansas who wanted to adopt in Brazil. They had been a family of five. They were driving with their three girls one day and got hit by another vehicle at an intersection. Two of the girls were instantly killed and Lana, who survived, was left with lifelong physical deficits and suffered from memory loss. Brad and Jolene were a great inspiration to me when I met them. In spite of their tragic story they were always happy, unselfish, and sensitive to others' pain.

It was very difficult to adopt from Brazil. There were horror stories about how the Americans adopted babies from there just to use their organs. Whether that ever happened I do not know, but to the Brazilian it was real. They made it almost impossible for those from other countries to adopt their children. But things were easing up enough that Brad and Jolene decided to take their chance. One of the requirements was that the parents-to-be had to spend thirty days living with the child in Brazil. Then they could either stay until it was all over or return home without their child until they were needed for the final paperwork and to take their child home.

Brad and Jolene wanted a younger child. A boy would have been great, but a girl was fine, too. They wanted to add to their almost empty nest. We got in contact with social services and they had two sweet girls, Diane, who was seven, and Danilla, who was five.They were full of spice and full of fun. They would live with us until the Koehns could come live with them for thirty days and again after that until the adoption papers were done. They adjusted well in spite of a past of neglect and being molested. We taught them English and they learned amazingly fast. They were so excited when Brad and Jolene came and stayed the thirty days with them. When they left for home it was with many tears and promises and many phone calls were made checking on progress.

Then came the day we all dreaded when the social worker called and said the girls' mom was able to get them back. The girls had been playing outside in the red dirt when we told them they had to come in for showers before they went back to their mom. Diane was the oldest and the quietest. She began to cry but went for her shower. Danilla did not just cry, she kicked and screamed and refused to go shower. With tears and prayers, I dragged her to the shower and got her cleaned up.

We were all so distressed that we all knelt to pray as we sobbed with grief. We gave the girls a Bible Story Book as a farewell gift. They could speak English well by then and we hoped they would remember all we had taught them.

We got in the car and started down the road. The girls clung to me as we drove to town. A dust storm came up as we drove and we had to stop beside the road once because we couldn't see ahead. Never had I seen such a storm ... in more ways than one.

It would be years before my parents would hear from the girls or see them again. Diane made contact with my parents when she was in her upper teens wanting to get reacquainted. She told them that Danilla was with their mom in another country and both were working as a prostitutes there.

Soon after the girls were sent back to their mother, we got a call that there was a baby boy for the Koehns. We picked him up at the birthing center. His mother was only a year older than me. I loved taking care of him. His crib was in my room and I had a doll to play with once again. He had the biggest mop of gorgeous black curls I had ever seen on a tiny baby. We had him for three months before it was time for the Koehns to come stay the thirty days. We were fostering SueEllen, a seven year old, also. She had been abused and lived on the streets rather than at home. She was a sweet child and did very well at first. Brad and Jolene came, gave both children all the love they could, and returned to Kansas to wait it out.

To our dismay, the Koehns got the dreaded call that their baby boy was suddenly wanted by his grandmother. With tears we again made the trip back to town to take the baby back.

During this all, another couple decided to try the Brazil adoption route. My uncle and aunt kept the baby until Ken and Dindy came from Michigan for their little Melissa. They stayed the thirty days, then Ken returned to his dairy in Michigan while Dindy stayed to wait the time out in Brazil. I would go spend nights with them after Ken left so she wouldn't be so alone. It was a time of much prayer and faith for them, knowing how things were not going so well for the other family. But to everyone's relief and joy, two months later the adoption was through and Dindy was flying back to Michigan with Melissa in her arms.

It was hard to understand why it went so well for some while for others all seemed to go awry. For the Koehns it just got worse. I wondered how much more they could take. What they call the "honey-moon" stage with foster children was over for SueEllen and our sweet girl began disappearing. She became sneaky and uncooperative. If I put myself in her shoes, I can see how she might have been feeling. She never got along with her mom, so she was sent to these people's house to live until she could go live somewhere else far away. She liked her new parents-to-be, but realistically, would she ever go live with them? Why would she believe it would be a forever home when our home was temporary? She began telling us she didn't want to go to the US to live with Brad and Jolene. Children are so afraid of rejection that they are afraid to love. We tried to reason with her and told her how wonderful it would be, but she was firm. One day I walked in the house and heard her on the phone telling her mom she wanted to go back to live with her! We knew that there was nothing left but to call the Koehns with the sad news once more. My parents met SueEllen again when she was only fifteen years old and she had a baby of her own!

Once more, we got a call from social services. This time they had a four year old boy who had too much energy for his aging grandmother. She was his only known relative. He was the sweetest little, big guy we ever did see. He had lived in an adult world and acted like one and was delightful to talk to. He was just so grown up. We had a lot of fun running through the house together, playing hide and seek, or jumping out at each other and tussling on the floor. My poor dad, who didn't enjoy so much extra noise, had some ear-plugging to do. The house rang with little Bruce's laughter in those months while we waited for the time the Koehns would come. They were so happy to have a boy. Their thirty days flew by and they left Bruce with many tears and prayers. And this time they were able to take their big guy home! They also adopted a little girl in the US so they were once again a family of five.

After I married and lived in South Dakota, the Koehns came by to see me. Bruce and I ended up in a tussle until my silly children began crying because they thought we were fighting, so we had to quit until they could understand it was all in fun. But whenever we saw each other we would have a tussle. That is, until Bruce got too much muscle for me to go up against.

CHAPTER 3

My life seemed to follow a path of "nevers." I was never going to teach school! But when I heard that the Mennonite school needed a middle grade teacher I suddenly knew I wanted to teach and I put in my application. I was seventeen with lots of energy and I knew my chances of getting the job were not high, as they liked a teacher to be no younger than eighteen. But to my surprise they hired me! I was excited and full of ideas, and I found that I loved teaching.

I was a Brazilian at heart and one thing I was never going to do was teach in the US. I was going to stay in Brazil where my heart was. But, such was my luck, I was sitting one day in my classroom and suddenly I knew I needed to go teach in the US. I was thinking it would be for at least one year, just so I could get new ideas and experience. I taught one more year in Brazil before I headed North to teach in a Mennonite school in Murray, Kentucky. I wrote a little vow and handed it to the school board. I wanted them to know just how much I loved my job. I wrote, "I take this school by my side to love and to cherish ... till a man doth us part," though I actually had no plans of a man parting us for years to come, and especially not a man from the North country.

When I was seventeen, before I had begun teaching in Brazil, I had made a trip to the US to try my wings and see what I could see. I'd gone with a strong determination that no one from the male species would woo me away from my beloved Brazil. I flew to the US with some friends, then I took off on my own, to California to see my oldest sister Denise and her family. A year or two before, they had moved from Brazil to California. It was wonderful to see Fred, Denise, and the kids again. Denise and I had a lot of catching up to do. Oh, and there were a couple guys she thought I should meet. They were good friends of theirs, lots of fun, and the story went on.

We went to a wedding the first Sunday I was there. I was innocently standing in line to go eat at the reception with my sister when this "good friend" of theirs was suddenly beside us. My sister introduced us, and from that moment on Pat only stopped teasing and "harassing" me, as he called it, long enough to apologize for all the harassment, just to start all over again. I told him with all that apologizing he was the "sorriest" guy I had ever met, but I liked him a lot more than I wanted to admit. And in spite of the constant harassment, he made me feel special and heard. I certainly was charmed by his attention, but had no plans of ever being more than "just friends." I was very careful not to actually say the word "never" about marrying him, but in my heart I was convinced it was a for sure "never." Well, I thought I was, anyways. There seemed to be a little confusion developing on the matter.

Pat made me furious one evening when the young people got together. Fred and Denise were youth advisers so they were there, too. I went looking for Denise and there she was talking in hushed tones to Pat. I had to know what they were saying so I got up close enough to hear. He was asking her if I had a boyfriend. That's all I needed to hear! I was completely outraged! I went up and told him some things were none of his business. I was so furious, I ignored him the rest of the evening. In the Mennonite church we belonged to at that time, courting was not permitted and feelings were not discussed openly between two interested people. It was a guessing game at it's best!

The next day I was feeling bad I had gotten so upset, especially after Denise let me know that an apology was in place. So, I did what I had never done before to any guy and called Pat, asking him to come over so I could talk to him. He lived just a few blocks away so he was there in a few minutes. I went out and sat in his pickup with him. I told him I was sorry I had gotten so upset and I was good with us being friends, but to rest assured that between him and I it would never be more than friendship! He drove away from there and said to himself, "God, deliver me from bold women!" We were like magnets with wrong sides to each other one minute and the next minute we were strangely drawn together.

Back in Brazil, in the middle of January, I received a birthday card and letter from him. My birthday was in July, but no matter. I was delighted to get a card from a "good friend." He wrote that he had moved to South Dakota. He didn't know when my birthday was, but here was the card. I had never received a letter from a guy. I let my dad read the letter and he made sure I knew that he would not put his blessings on a correspondence with this "friend" of mine. That was a nice fix to be in! Though I enjoyed exchanging words with Pat more than anyone else I knew and he was the best "guy friend" I had ever had, I respected my dad enough that I didn't mail the letter I had written to Pat.

I went to Murray, KY to teach when I was nineteen. I was geared to teach and mostly kept my mind on the job at hand, but I was feeling bad for Pat that I hadn't sent at least a note in return to his friendly letter. So, I called Denise and asked her to let him know my silence was due to my dad's request and not because I meant to ignore him.

She passed the message on for me and I tried to forget the whole thing and focus on my teaching. I taught with two fun gals, Diana and Connie. Diana was Brazilian by birth. She was adopted in Brazil by an American family who had once lived there. When she was still young they returned to the US.

She was just a little older than me, and in spite of warnings from others that her and I would likely be too headstrong to get along, we became fast friends and had a great time.

Connie was like a big sister to us. She was a good sport and did a great job of taking me to town and other places I needed to go, as I had no car.

Then one day my sister called me up and said that she thought Pat was seriously looking my way and I told her to tell him to look the *other* way. But Denise said it wasn't fair to not give a guy a chance like that. You don't say "no" until you're asked. That made some sense. She said she thought he might be calling me to chat. Oh, boy!

During this time I felt Jesus very near and was enjoying a deepening relationship with Him. In Him I found all my joy and happiness. I look back and realize God was preparing me for one of the biggest decision I would make in my life. I waited for the dreaded, yet longed for phone call. I, personally, was ready with buckets of cold water.

He didn't call. He wrote me a letter. It took me completely off guard because you can't argue with a letter. Seeing as, in the Holdeman Mennonite church, the man does not normally propose personally to the lady he wishes to marry, nor do they allow courtship, I wasn't surprised that his letter was kept to just simple chit chat. Although, I did read more into a couple comments than he intended. It was enough to make me want to run, though I knew not to where. But I ran to him instead of away from him when I went to California for Christmas and, to my secret delight, he did, too!

I arrived in California late in the evening, tired and ready to go to bed. Pat was going Christmas caroling with the youth and called to see if I would join them. I felt honored, but chose the comfort of my niece's bed over the fun of caroling. It was Saturday night, I was exhausted, and I wanted to be rested for church in the morning.

To say I was nervous when I got to church is an understatement! I just didn't know when Pat would suddenly appear and I didn't know how I was going to handle him, so I was glad he was nowhere to be seen before church, yet a little disappointed. I sat with Denise and suddenly she jabbed me with her elbow and whispered, "There goes your future husband," as Pat walked down the aisle to sit down. She didn't get beat up only because we were sitting in church. I was so nervous and my stomach doing so many flips that my hands were literally dripping sweat. I had a problem with sweaty hands and feet all my life and I couldn't get the faucet to shut off, nor the butterflies to settle.

I made it through church somehow. After the service, Denise introduced me to her friends and to Pat's parents. I tried to be ready for Pat when he came over to say hi, but my heart was coming up my throat. The first thing he said when he shook my hand was something about my wet hands. Of course he would notice! He had that way of noticing everything and I was afraid he could see right through me. Somehow, he made the room feel too full, but after he walked away the room felt unbearably empty. I just needed this roller coaster I was on to stop so I could get off and run.

Over the next few days I got very sick with some kind of a chest virus. My sister's gentle touch hadn't changed over the years. She took care of me and my niece who joined me on the sick bed. It was almost fun to be sick. I couldn't remember the last time I had been waited on hand and foot with no place to go and no responsibilities. Except for intense pain in my throat and chest, it was relaxing. And I had all the time in the world to go on my runaway emotional rides.

I called Diana just to see if she could help me sort out my emotions. I could barely talk but croaked out all my heart troubles and she said, "I think you're falling in love." All I could answer was, " I just don't know."

We had planned to go to the coast and spend the day at the wharf. I woke up on the Thursday morning we had planned to go and evaluated the situation. I was physically not in the best shape, but maybe OK enough to go. To stay home would have been pure agony, because Pat and another friend of Denise's would be going along. Besides, I had been having some unusual conversations with God. The day before I had told God that I would not marry Pat no matter what, so on Thursday morning I was shocked to find myself telling God that I didn't care what He said, but I had to marry Pat because I just couldn't live without him. I just prayed God understood my crazy conversations with Him because I sure didn't!

So, away we went. I had my pillow and blanket and a shadow of a voice I once had. Pat harassed me without mercy and I could only glare back at him.

It was cold when we got to Monterey and I was glad for the bowl of clam chowder at the wharf that helped warm me a bit. The wind was so cold it made my chest just ache and I realized that anyone who was making decisions with their brain instead of with their heart would have been home in bed. When we all went on a boat ride I found myself standing at the front of the boat with Pat as we sliced through the waves. It was exhilarating to stand so near him and at that moment I knew my heart and I never wanted to leave his side.

To my utter frustration the next day when he came to say goodbye, before he left for South Dakota, I was actually glad to see him go. My one regret was that I hadn't gotten a chance to give him my carefully prepared "only friends" lecture.

I went back to Kentucky a few days later, still weak from all my chest and heart viruses. Revival meetings had begun and I was not enjoying them. I guess I had done too much telling God what I was going to do instead of asking Him and for all my telling I was seemingly as clueless as ever about what I really wanted. Diana was going through her own trip down Lovesick Lane, so we understood each other's misery completely.

One evening while getting ready for church, my heart was so heavy I just begged God to tell me what He wanted me to do and I would do whatever He asked of me, even if it was to just forget about Pat. I was so relieved to find the fight was over! I finally felt the calm that comes after a storm and went to church at peace that evening.

I got home and went to bed still feeling like a bird let out of a cage. I lay there thanking God for His goodness and guidance when suddenly I found my mind wandering over to Pat way over in South Dakota. I wanted to scream! I was over this Pat obsession! He was just the best guy friend I had ever had. And who marries friends? It took me a long time to fall asleep!

I was sitting at my desk the next day in my classroom while my students were quietly studying. They were a good bunch of kids, so I had time to sit and think about all my heart trouble for a bit. I looked out the window searching the landscape as though I would find an answer out there. I was struggling and arguing the same old things all over again and I knew I just couldn't go on like this. My main problem was telling Pat, "No." I couldn't bear to break his heart. I was so blind, I could not see that that is love itself, to care that much about someone else. I had been looking for answers in the wrong places. I heaved a big sigh and looked up and told God what He knew I would say all along, "OK, God, I'll marry him."

And to my joy, the roller coaster stopped and I ran! But this time it wasn't away from Pat.

Denise was happy with my news and she promptly called Pat and told him of my declaration of love for him. Pat was in a state of shock. Though he had liked me and enjoyed being with me more than any other girl he knew, he had not sorted through his feelings enough to be sure he wanted to settle down yet. He had run every time things had gotten serious with a girl before. He talked to his sister, Jill. She only laughed and said, "Oh, Pat, you finally got caught!" Finding no sympathy there, he went to the pastor and his wife and they listened with great amusement and said, "Aha, you got caught this time." He pleaded with them to tell him he wouldn't have to get serious about marriage yet. He was going for his own roller coaster ride, for which I will always be smugly and completely pleased. The funny thing was that they were having revivals in South Dakota at this time, and Pat was a song leader. His congregation loved to pick a song at revivals that was normally sung at weddings. Twice it was selected and Pat had to lead it. God has a sense of humor, I'm sure, and so did the minister's wife. She just sat and smirked at Pat whenever he looked her way. He was getting no help from her, and his beautiful bachelorhood was being threatened.

Finally, one day as he was driving along, he realized the fight was over and said, "OK, God, I'll marry her."

Meanwhile, I had no idea all this was going on. I was just glad I was ready when he would send the big question. I always have said we got together on a misunderstanding, because had I known he was actually not letting himself think seriously about our relationship, I would have never let myself do so either. But God knew what it would take to get two stubborn people together. And I will say, my sister has never accepted any part of the blame for all this. She must have skipped math in school.

I was ready when my pastor called and wanted me to come over for a talk. I knew what was coming of course, because Pat had called me and let me know that he had talked to his pastor and asked him to send me his marriage proposal. My answer was quickly relayed back to him. That night, we talked for a full four hours on the phone.

In April I flew to South Dakota for Easter to see Pat and the land where I would be living. We made wedding plans and decided to have our wedding in California where we had met. I enjoyed getting to know his sister Jill, her husband, Dave, and their baby, Luke.

My parents came to Kentucky when school was out and together we went to Kansas to see our relatives, then on to California for our wedding. The Holdeman Mennonite custom is to have the wedding in the bride's congregation, but Pat had been laid off from his job and I had used up all my money on dentist bills and the like, so having our wedding in Brazil seemed an impossibility.

I was so glad my brother Carlos and his family came for our wedding. It was hard for me to not have so many of my friends and family there. The majority of our guests were strangers to me.

On the morning of our wedding, I stayed and waited for Pat to come pick me up after everyone else had gone to church. He came and I noticed he was a bit nervous about the big day ahead. He said he wanted to pray together before we went, so we knelt together and asked for God's guidance and blessings on our day.

Our wedding service was nice, but we both wished that we could have had a simple little ceremony with just a few guests instead of a big trditional wedding. We were not given a choice, so big traditional wedding it was. We got married and that is what counts. We were so glad when we finished opening our last gift at the reception and could get ourselves away from the crowd and be alone.

We headed for the beautiful California coast feeling like birds set free. We spent our honeymoon walking the wharfs and beaches, just enjoying each other, laughing, and dreaming of our future together while Pat sang Beach Boy love songs to me in between the harrassments.

CHAPTER 4

We lived in South Dakota for the next seven years. Lissandra was born a couple years after we were married. I thought that was a nice way to start a family, with a girl first. I had secretly hoped it would be a girl all along. Sometimes I definitely feel that God enjoys giving us just what we want and spoiling us a little. Not in a bad way, but just like a daddy would give his little girl something she really wants just cause He loves her. And other times He gives us just what He knows will fulfill us the most, and it may not exactly be what we wished for. He is just good that way!

When Lissandra was nearly a year I began thinking a playmate for her would be nice. Pat wasn't too sure what the rush was, but he was a good sport and soon we were planning for our next child.

I have never regretted having Marcio so soon after Sandi, as we often called her. Though I nearly had him even sooner than we expected. It was an honest mistake, really. I got the nesting syndrome and had to have my house cleaned top to bottom and I had it pretty much done, but I still had the top of some of the living room walls to do. I got on a chair to reach as high as possible, but there were a few inches close to the ceiling I just couldn't quite touch. I went and got Sandi's little bench she used to stand on at the sink. I was thirty-three weeks along and big enough that I should have known better, but I couldn't leave that little bit unwashed. I put the bench on the folding chair and carefully climbed up. I hate heights, so I was getting out of my comfort zone with this daring but necessary maneuver. I used the wall for support and, tada! I could reach!

Pat was in the sun room that he used for an office. There was a big picture window between the office and living room. Pat could see me slaving away from his cozy perch on his chair by the computer. I was getting a little miffed at him for not having as much cleaning zeal as I had. Well, I'd show him I could do it. I scrubbed like a true nester will.

I must have tried to reach an extra inch further, instead of getting down from my scaffolding and moving it over, as I cleaned over the picture window. Suddenly, the floor rose up to meet my left side and my feet simultaneously flew closer to the ceiling. I don't know if Pat took his eyes off of his computer long enough to see his dear, beloved, hard working wife fly past him to hit with a great thud or not. But the earthquake quality of the thud, along with the sound of a great something hitting the floor, brought him on the run.

By the time he got there I had already done my calculations. This faster than normal descent was definitely his fault. Had he helped like a nice, loving husband I wouldn't be checking for broken bones right then.

When he inquired after my well being I let him know how well I wasn't, thanks to him. Of course, he didn't follow my train of thought at all. He spied the bench that was dangling from the chair and looked at me in disbelief. I was soon forgetting my husbands sins, though, as I began to worry about how the baby was handling this unexpected jolt.

Pat immediately called my doctor and explained in detail about a bench and a chair and a deranged wife. Could she help? She could help! We got ourselves over to her office on the double so she could check out the baby.

She listened to the heart beat. All sounded fine. But to be safe I needed to go up to he hospital to check if there were contractions and make sure I wasn't going into premature labor. The nurses in OB were great. They remembered me from when Lissandra was born. Except that now they couldn't quit talking about benches on chairs and could I come clean their houses, too?

We left in good spirits. There were no signs of contractions and all was well.

Until we got halfway home on our twenty minute drive. That's when the contractions began.

We timed them and they were strong enough for discomfort at five minutes apart. We called the doctor. She said to get right back to the hospital. They hooked me up to their contraction reader machine and the heart monitor to track the baby's heartbeat. The doctor ordered a sonogram and did we want to know if it was a boy or girl? We decided we wanted to know. It was a boy! Just what I had ordered!

They gave me medication to stop the contractions. Junior was not allowed out until he was thirty-six weeks along at least. I was told I had three weeks of bed rest ahead of me. It sounded like three months. I really thought it was partly a joke until the doctor said I couldn't lift Lissandra or get up for anything except necessary matters and I could take sponge baths.

What? Sponge baths?

This wasn't turning out to be any fun at all. And I was to leave all dirt alone until after Junior came. I could do all the cleaning I wanted then.

I was good and lay on the couch on the first day. Friends brought food so I wouldn't have to cook. It was a real act of kindness and bravery on their part, as they were scared Pat wouldn't like what they brought. His being a picky eater is a quality that would drive most wives crazy, but my dad had been picky, too, so I just learned to live around it. Pat survived just fine!

Day two was not so easy. I couldn't lie on my sore side so my other side soon got weary of the endless job of warming the couch. I love to read, but it's somehow not as fun when that's all you have to do. Lissandra wouldn't come near me. She was leery of me ever since she had seen me hooked up to the monitors at the hospital. She was keeping a safe distance.

Day three, I was depressed. Three weeks seemed to stretch into years. I was near tears and Pat could hardly bear to watch me. Finally, I just sat up and said that was it. I would not lay there a minute longer. I would be careful and would rest if I felt the contractions were warming up.

We didn't tell the doctor. What happens at home stays at home. Marcio was born only one week before his due date. He was darker than Lissandra and full of dark peach fuzz on his forehead and ears. Needless to say, I felt wonderful after I was finally free of that little guy kicking around inside me and weighing me down. Lissandra was in big sister heaven. She had a real baby to hold all she wanted and she never tired of it.

My baby fever was quieted and I was going to sit back and enjoy my two little ones. Which I did ... but to our great joy we found out we had another little one to look forward to when Marcio was only six months old. I was in no hurry for that pregnancy to end. I had so much to do and enjoy before more enjoyment came along.

During this time, we helped Jill and Dave run a restaurant in the small town of Iroquois and Marcio and Lissandra were there a lot with us. The waitresses carried them on their hips as they served customers and they got far more attention than is possibly needed to raise a child. When they would snitch fries from the customers' plates we would tell them not to. But the customers would say, "Sure, they could!" and for us to just let them be. You can guess who the kids listened to.

Meanwhile, I was definitely pregnant. I waitressed and helped with whatever needed doing. There were days I went home after work so tired I thought I couldn't move one more step, but somehow I bathed the children and put them to bed and got myself into bed. I would lie there and just ache all over. This third pregnancy seemed more difficult and I was easily irritated. I really felt sorry for those who had to be near me.

During this third and last pregnancy, Pat and I did some serious talking. I had a dream of adoption being part of our family plan. Pat was not so sure about it, but we both realized that at the rate I was able to have children there would soon be no room for adopting. I knew without a doubt that God had placed this special desire to adopt in my heart. The reason this came up was because it was best to do a tubal right after a birth. Plus, it was much cheaper, and we didn't have a spare penny. So, what to do?

Pat finally told me he was neutral on the matter and would leave the decision up to me. He was still not saying he agreed with adopting later, but in my heart of hearts I knew he'd come around. I prayed fervently to God to help me know what was best. I was only twenty-five at the time, as my doctor made sure I knew. She went over all the what-ifs with me so I could look at all angles before I made a decision. She did her job well, but my mind was settled. God has a special plan for each family and I knew He had a very special one for ours. And I found that when God came along with His plan it was always more exciting, more perfect, and more satisfying than anything we could plan or dream. As it was, though, I had very little time for dreaming.

Life was happening and I found myself once more heading for the hospital. Rafael was born five days after the twin towers fell. It was all anyone could talk about. Rafael was as fair as Marcio had been dark. He had reddish blonde hair, which didn't surprise me. God knows I love variety. I felt so fulfilled with my little family and yet so tired. I was a very busy mama. But I found time to make a quilt, put puzzles together, sew for me and Lissandra, read to my little ones, and run to town with Pat when he needed to get something. And I still was putting many hours in at the cafe. My little engine was being run hard ... maybe a little too hard.

CHAPTER 5

Economy had a say in the changes that came to our lives next. As the economy took a slump, so did the restaurant business in our small town. What made things go really bad for us was the fact that we lived in a community of farmers with old time values. They believed that if money is tight, you tighten your belt, and guess what? You quit eating out! Business was so slow that Pat got himself a side job at the Pepsi plant where he literally watched Pepsi bottles go by on a belt for hours each day. It was truly the worst job he ever endured. His nature is one that likes interaction with people and he loves action. He nearly went crazy during this time and I almost went with him.

Then one day, he got a call from a former co-worker in California who said he was quitting his job as restaurant manager to be a full time real estate agent. He wondered if Pat wanted the restaurant job. We had not entertained any serious thoughts or ideas of living in CA. I had seen the congestion and endless flow of humanity and I didn't want to live in all that buzz, nor did Pat really, athough it would be like going back home for him. We were in shock at first, but the more we thought about how good it would be to have a reliable income, the more CA looked like it maybe wasn't too crowded to fit us in. Pat knew he would like the job and we both knew we would love to be by his parents. He put in his application at the restaurant and soon got a call back. They interviewed him by phone. Then they paid for his ticket to fly to CA for the next two interviews. They liked him and said they would call him in a few days with their decision. He flew back to SD and we began packing.

Pat's parents offered that we could live with them until their place sold. They were selling their house and land to a developer. The house would be available for us to live in until it was torn down to clear the land for a subdivision. We were set to go!

And then we got the call that the restaurant decided not to hire as they would have someone already working there take over management.

We were suddenly high and dry again. What did God have in mind? It had seemed like an open door to move, but now what would we do? Reality was that the door was closing for us to stay in South Dakota.

If one door closes another must open. We prayed fervently for direction and it seemed like moving ahead was better than staying and going backwards.

Pat called a man he had worked for in almond harvesting in CA and asked if he had work for him for the fall. He got the job instantly. We now had lodging and a temporary job. Beyond that, it was up to God.

We left early one morning and headed west. I felt adventurous. Pat felt a fair bit of pessimism; one all faith and hope, the other all gloom and doom. Would it really work out? Would he find a good job after harvest?

" Relax, relax, relax," quoth I, "God has never left us stranded yet."

And indeed He didn't. After harvest, we found an add in the paper for a job as a construction site superintendent. Pat had worked in construction before in California so that stood him in good stead. He had little else to show except experience, but they hired him! God had a plan just as I was sure He did.

We lived with Pat's mom and dad for six months before they moved to their new home. It is a very dear memory I have, living with them and seeing our children enjoy their grandparents. Lissandra was five, Marcio three, and Rafael two. They were running over with life. They entertained each other and played amazingly well together. I began wondering if Rafael would benefit from having a younger sibling. He was so strong willed and sometimes someone younger to look out for can help mellow a child out. I figured that if we started the adoption process he would have at least a year, if not more, before he had to give up the title of "the baby."

I talked to Pat and he was still dragging his feet. Lissandra was begging me to get started finding her a baby sister. She was a very persistent child. She finally asked me why her daddy didn't want to find her a sister and I told her that I wondered if her daddy was being just a bit selfish about it all, but he just wasn't ready yet. And I explained to her that it wouldn't work to go through the adoption process if the parents weren't both sure that this was what they wanted to do. She understood what I was saying, but didn't like my answer. She went to her daddy and asked him why he was being selfish and not letting her have a little sister. He told me later that her question had gone straight to his heart because he knew he did not have a good reason for not adopting. He said I could look for an agency, but it had to be one that we could afford.

We were both sure we didn't want to foster. It would have been too emotionally upsetting to our little children to become attached to a baby, only to face the possibility of giving her up again. I had been given the name of a Christian adoption agency, so I called them. The cost was very high and I didn't like their approach. Besides, the lady I talked to said the chances of us getting a baby through them were low, because we already had three children.

I was disappointed. I was looking for an agency that had more of an open mind. She was kind enough to give me some phone numbers for other agencies that might be more suitable for us. I began on the list right away. I felt my heart sinking lower and lower as they all said about the same thing and were not what we could afford. All of them except one, where the receptionist said that she was not able to talk at the moment, but she would call me back later.

I don't know how God could have so much patience with me. I had spent two hours making phone calls and hadn't found what I was looking for, so I was ready to despair. It never entered my mind that there were other days and other contacts I could make. Nope, not me. I took my heavy heart to my bedside and knelt down and told God my problem. I asked Him to help me find just the right agency, one we could afford and was open minded. I told Him that He would have to be the one showing us the right agency because I didn't know where to begin. I was out of phone numbers to call. I got up feeling better about it all. God was the one deciding who and where, so I could relax. It was my turn to just relax, relax.

A little before 5 pm, the phone rang. I answered and it was the receptionist calling me back. She told me they were a non-profit Christian agency and that us having three children already made no difference to them. The total cost was very small compared to the other agencies. I was so excited. I knew, without a doubt, that this was the agency I had asked God for. I was suddenly glad for the long, but really not long, delay in getting an answer. If there hadn't been the delay I wouldn't have gone and prayed so urgently for God's help. I just needed to know God was the one in control.

God knew I would need that special blessing and assurance again and again in the coming journey we were to take. It proved to be a journey longer and rockier than we ever could have imagined.

CHAPTER 6

As humans, we have a tendency to think the future will be pretty much like the present. That was the mindset I had after the return phone call. I was hopeful all would go quickly and smoothly. The person I spoke with at Family Connections Adoption Agency was very helpful and said she would send us a packet of information. She also said they always started adoption classes in March. It was February when I called, so we only had a few weeks to wait to get started. I dreaded the paperwork part of it, but at the same time was eager to take the first step forward.

Family Connections was an agency started by a lady who adopted children herself, including two with Down syndrome. She decided to use her knowledge and experience to help other families have successful adoptions.

She started out with her first office in a church basement. She struggled through a lot of red tape and legalities. But her business grew until she had to move to a bigger place. The office we went to in Modesto was pretty new. It had been twenty years since she had first opened office. She had offices in two or three other cities also. Her policy was to make adoption "matches" that were best for the parents and the children.

Family Connections helped families adopt children from the foster care system in California, and from several countries. It was a bit scary for us to adopt through the foster system, but they quickly assured us that out of 2,700 adoptions, only four children had returned to the birth parents. The adopting parents had known it was a very risky adoption, but had tried anyways. The children Family Connections dealt with were children who were ready to be placed in permanent homes and the State had done everything to make it work for the birth parent or parents before ending the parental rights.

We right away loved the family atmosphere at Family Connections. We soon learned to love them all and recognize their voices over the phone. When we began our classes we all wanted to know how long we should expect to wait before we would be matched with a child or children. They said the average wait time was about nine months, just like a pregnancy. Worst case might be a two year wait. The younger the child you wanted to adopt, the more you could expect to wait. They told us to keep an open mind. Sometimes parents met children much older than they had thought they wanted to adopt, fell in love, and adopted them.

We began working on our home studies, the physicals, fingerprints, and endless other little things. They set up payments for us in a way that it never seemed too hard to handle. I impatiently wanted to get it all done the first week, but it took us until July to complete everything, including private interviews for both Pat and me. The lady who started the agency always interviewed the parents-to-be. Her faith in God and her positive attitude inspired us. I shared my dreams with her. Years before, I had read in a Reader's Digest about a small town in Texas that had banded together and had given homes to quite a few African-American children. It was a beautiful story. I had always admired darker-skinned people and had often wished I had been darker. I suppose some of that came from wishing I would pass more easily as a Brazilian. So, we put in our paperwork that our first choice was a baby girl (it just made sense to have another girl), preferrably African-American, but we would consider any and every nationality. We were given a binder filled with pictures of waiting children. Some parents found their children this way. They made many matches by parents falling in love with those smiling little faces in the photos. I looked at and loved many of them. We would mark the ones we wanted our social worker to make inquiries about for us. Also, our social worker would send out our home study to all the children's social workers.

Then if they had a child they thought might fit well into our family, they would contact our social worker and she would in turn call us to see if we were interested.

Many times we would ask about a baby and the answer would come back that they had already been matched. Sometimes we would get a call asking if we would take a sibling group. We would agonize over it and wish we could say yes, but we knew we just weren't ready for that.

We also went to Adoption Picnics. The first one was so exciting. We had high hopes of meeting our little daughter. We were given instructions on how to behave ourselves. No asking personal questions to the children about their parents or foster parents. There was a fifteen minute limit for time spent with a child or sibling group. We were to interact with all age groups and, above all else, make sure the children were having fun. Only parents who had completed all their paperwork and were ready to adopt were allowed at these picnics. It was the same for the children. They had to be ready to be placed in permanent homes to be there.

We met at a beautiful park with huge trees and green lawns with the picnic area roped off. I guess it was to prevent anyone from just walking up and taking a child and to set the boundaries of where the children had to stay. After we had lunch together, they set up tables loaded with crafts. Small games were organized. Soon, there were bubbles floating on the breeze and kids running around with butterflies and other creatures painted on their faces. Parents set about making friends with the children and making sure they all had something to do and were having a good time. We were nervous and anxious and wondered how the children felt. You could see it in the older ones eyes; that questioning look. Will this one take me home? They would ask if we had other children at home and how many. They were told not to get too personal with us, but kids are kids. They need answers.

We played with two beautiful children, boy and girl, ages seven and eight. We hit it off and just wished we could take them home with us. Their eyes were so hopeful and pleading.

After about an hour of organized chaos we were done. Those that had a child or children they were interested in needed to fill out a paper and their social worker would talk with them and decide if they were a match or not. We had shown some interest in a baby girl we had seen, but had not had time to play with. We found out she had two siblings. Their social worker told us we didn't offer an African-American child enough. Love just wasn't enough. We had to offer them their culture. It needed to be taught to them and we needed to make sure they attended special holiday events with other African-Americans. Our small Mennonite society would not be enough.

We went to a second picnic with much less enthusiasm. It was fast becoming far from our favorite thing to do. We showed interest in a baby girl, but her social worker wasn't interested in the two hour drive to our house for visits. So, that was that!

We hit the two year wait time and had to renew our paper work. It was easier than starting from scratch, but no fun just the same. It did give us the feeling of doing something, at least. Then I hit a mental low due to some other circumstances in our life at the time, one of which was strong opposition from the pastors at the church we belonged to. They did not support our decision to adopt. We did not understand why and they did not explain their reasons to us. We turned to God in our anguish. We knew He was the only one that we could depend on in our distress. We had been taught that what the pastor said was pretty much the final word and should be followed. To go against them was a serious infraction and could end up in them excluding us from their group. We did not want this, but we didn't know how to comply without rejecting what God was asking us to do.

I finally found the courage to talk it over with our social worker before she went on maternity leave and handed our case over to another worker. She was very kind to me and suggested we put everything on hold for a while to catch our breath and help ease the pressure. We took her up on it and took a break.

Then, suddenly, construction slowed down and even came to a halt in many places. The company Pat worked for was building less and less houses and then it became evident that it was shutting down completely. Before long, Pat was given his severance pay. He decided to start up his own handyman business. It was a hard pull for us as we worked to build up a new business.

When it was time to move out of the old family house we found a delightful little house out in the country. We had a wonderful landlord, whom Pat's family had known for years. He asked us to landscape the yard and paint the interior of the house in exchange for rent. So, when we started our new business venture he was very long suffering and understanding when things got tight for us. I am ever and always amazed at God's care for His children. When things get tough there seems to always appear an angel in everyday clothes to help us along.

CHAPTER 7

When Pat was laid off in December, we decided to fly to Mississippi before starting our new business to visit his parents, who were there for two years managing a Mennonite nursing home. It was close to where Pat's youngest sister, Beth, lived so we would stay with them and all be together for Christmas, including his sister, Jill, and her family. It was bound to be fun. Beth and her husband, Marc, had been unable to have children and had chosen to adopt. They had been matched to a cute little guy and were waiting for all the paperwork to get through to go pick him up in Guatemala.

We had Christmas dinner at the nursing home with the few residents who were not gone to spend the day with their families. It was a quiet, beautiful day.

Dave and Jill had some hunters that stayed at their house in South Dakota during pheasant season, who had a condo on Orange Beach in Alabama. They offered that Dave could use their condo for a few days in the winter and we were condo-on-Orange-Beach-bound the next day. It was lovely to arrive at a sunny beach after days of cloudy weather in Mississippi. We each found quarters suitable for our little families and settled in to enjoy beach life for three short days.

I was out walking the beach as often as I could. The first day it was a bit cool, but it slowly got warmer. The beach had more shells and driftwood than the California beaches. I noticed people gathered shells and there were some who found sand dollars. They were pretty sand dollars, too. They were a different design than the ones on the west coast. Inside they had tiny white things that looked like angels or doves in flight.

At first, I didn't get too involved in gathering the pretty things in the sand. I figured they would end up being dust collectors at my house, so why bother? But I found myself becoming addicted as the children brought me their treasures, even though I wasn't sure how we would get them all packed up in our bags and flown home with us. I was soon making my own collection and became enthused with the amount of sand dollars people were finding and started looking in earnest for one for myself.

As I walked, I began talking to God about the ache in my heart. I talked to Him about all the opposition we were facing with adopting, both with the pastors and with the social workers. The long wait was beginning to look like it would never end. I felt Him beside me as I told Him my frustrations.

I had so many questions. What was His message to us? Had we misunderstood Him? Was it time to say we had tried and it just wasn't for us? My heart cried out to Him for answers. I knew for sure we did not want to enter into an adoption without it being one hundred percent in His plan. I unloaded two-and-a-half years of frustrations and questions on Him. His nearness brought so much comfort to me. He was so near it felt like I could have reached out and touched Him.

My eyes were constantly searching the sand. I reached down and turned over shells, hoping to find my sand dollar underneath. I came to a place where hundreds of sand dollars washed up on a ledge. I was pretty sure I would find one there. I looked for a long time, but the water washed them up with such force against the ledge that they were all broken. Some were ground to tiny bits, others were just partially broken. But not one was complete.

I finally found one the size of a nickel with just a little chip out of it, but I specifically wanted a medium size one that was not chipped or broken. I had, in my talking to God, been begging Him to help me find a sand dollar even while I begged Him to show us what to do with our adoption. I was not conscious of how it happened, but my desire to have a lovely sand dollar in my hand and to know He would place a baby in my arms became one prayer. I knew God delights in our asking. So, I asked. I knew He could give me one as easily as the other.

Night was approaching so I gave up the search until the next day. The next day was the last day on the beach. I would look for my sand dollar until I found it. I had so much hope that God would help me find one. He could hide them all from me as easily as He could show me ten of them.

After breakfast I went to the beach again while the men and boys went to an airplane museum. The little girls played together, so I was on my own. I took up where I had left off the day before. It was a beautiful morning; clear skies with a slight breeze. Life was good. I had all day to search for my answer.

I was again conscious of God's nearness as we walked. I met a lady who had found three small, but perfect sand dollars all in one spot. I had this feeling that God was trying me out. Three for one, but none for me. Then it came to me that our adoption story had been the same. People all around us were having children placed in their arms and for them it looked so easy. They put out their hands and, behold, there were the children they had asked for. But for us it had been a long, hard search that yielded nothing but heartache. Would that be the end of our story?

I went in for lunch and had a short nap. I had precious few hours left for sand dollar searching, so I went out to make hay while the sun shone. My zeal increased and I even had some helpers. But I knew in my heart of hearts that I had to find it with my own eyes or it wouldn't hold my answer.

As evening came nearer I ventured further out. I would turn back soon, but kept going farther and farther. I realized my chances were about over, so I began begging God to just help me be happy without a sand dollar. To be a happy wife and mother without my baby. I plead in earnest. It was becoming final. All I asked for was joy in my dark hour. Joy in my God and not in my circumstances. He was so near. If I had Him, what more did I need? I just wanted His arms around me while I came to grips with my disappointment. It had been a journey of many lessons learned. He had shown us rainbows when it seemed all was dark and stormy. Others had to give up more. I could be happy.

I saw the sun was touching the water. I needed to go back so I wasn't out in the dark alone.

Alone? I certainly didn't feel alone.

I turned back but would hold onto hope as long as the sun put out its last golden rays. I looked closely where I walked. I kicked aside little piles of shells and hoped my eye would catch something it had missed on my way out. Maybe. Then I realized the sun was going fast and I had not stopped to see the beauty of it. So, I stopped and just looked as it sent its orange glow over the water.

I was drinking it in when I suddenly realized a wave was coming and I was in its path. I stepped back, still watching the sunset reflected on the water. Then my gaze was drawn to the wave as it rolled back into the ocean. As I watched, my eyes caught sight of a small white object tumbling in the water at my feet. I sucked in my breath as I reached down to grab it before it slid back in the ocean.

It was my answer and it was perfect. Not one blemish, not one crack or chip. Just perfect. Not too small and not too big. My eyes filled with tears and my heart overflowed with awe at what my loving Father would do for one of His children. I almost expected to see His big, strong hand or one of His angels standing there after dropping my sand dollar at my feet. My heart was full as I continued back to my family.

I asked God what it all meant and His message was clear: "I will give you your child the same way I gave you the sand dollar. You will need to go to 'the beach' to look. But you won't need to dig or turn anything upside down looking. I will put your baby in your arms and you will know when you have found your 'sand dollar.'"

I felt like I was walking on air on my way back to the condo. With a promise like that, I could wait however long it would take.

I just couldn't wait to tell Pat.

CHAPTER 8

While in Mississippi, some friends told us about a book they had read. It explained how the Devil hates for us to succeed and will mercilessly try to spoil our lives. But prayer in the name of Jesus has great power and when we pray God sends His angels to fight the evil spirits working against us. If we get discouraged and don't pray, it gives the Devil more power.

A strong desire came over me, after reading this book, to pray for our baby. I, of course, had been praying all along, but my prayers had been that God would help us find our baby. It came to me strongly that the Devil had no desire to see us find a child that we would give love and happiness to. He was working against us. So, for the month of January I begged God to take the evil one's power away so he could not come near our baby and that he would have no power over our adoption. My prayers were filled with such a great urgency and I prayed from the depths of my being.

We struggled through the usual ups and downs of starting a new business that year. But, thanks to our loving Father, Pat found work to keep him busy, though at times it seemed the evil forces were trying to make everything go wrong in that area, too. After a while, Pat fell into more of a routine and we began enjoying a more steady income. Even though we were making just barely enough to put food on the table, we enjoyed Pat being self employed. Our landlord was a very kind man and allowed us to work off our rent when we could not pay him money for it. We thanked God for this many times.

Then we got a call from our social worker that there was an adoption fair coming up. We hadn't been to one of those and decided to go. They had social workers there with photos and information at their booths of children in their area waiting to be chosen for adoption. So, if we saw any child that caught our eye, they could answer our questions and we could possibly be matched.

I was kind of excited about this way of doing things because then there wasn't that dread in my heart of seeing the pain and longing in the children's eyes when they realized we wouldn't be giving them their forever home. There was a laughing face in one photo of a little boy that caught my fancy.

"No," said Pat, "we're looking for a girl."

The social worker also made sure I noticed the little guy's ears. They were low and that meant he probably had FAS (fetal alcohol syndrome). I thought it strange that a social worker was trying to discourage me instead of encourage me. Oh, well. Maybe next time we went "to the beach" we'd find our baby girl. She didn't seem to be at this place.

Sometimes we wondered if our agency was about ready to give up hope of us ever being matched. They had never had parents wait three years for a baby. They never showed us that they were discouraged and we certainly could find no fault in them for how slow things had gone. We just knew God had a reason for the long wait. He was preparing a very special child for us. Little did we know how very special and wonderful.

Meanwhile, God was preparing us. I became more and more baby hungry. I had not really felt that empty arm feeling and had worried about it. But I think God knew the wait would have been truly unbearable if I had had that to deal with, too.

Don't misunderstand! I wanted another child, but a mother usually gets that longing to hold her child and I had long awaited this feeling of needing my arms filled. It developed in a very healthy fashion and I was pretty sure we would soon find our "sand dollar."

In September, there was another adoption picnic we could attend down in Oakland at the zoo. I figured I could surely at least find a monkey there. We went to "the beach" just in case our sand dollar was there. The children had come with social workers and foster moms earlier that morning and gone through the zoo. We parents came in time for orientation and lunch at the shelter in the zoo's park.

It was just a bad day. I was exhausted and my emotions and mental state were close to reaching the "out of control" state. We were encouraged to sit with others from our agency. I was glad for that. It was refreshing to swap stories and have something in common in a room full of strangers. The social worker doing the orientation was having a hard time making the afternoon ahead of us sound fun. She hollered rules out to us in no uncertain terms. You about expected to see one of those long, black batons hanging from her waist that cops wear, and if you didn't mind the rules you'd get whacked. Pat looked at me and wondered if we should maybe not stay for very long. There just wasn't a "picnic" mood and it was looking like a waste of our time to come. But we decided to try and stick it out for a while. There were going to be children there ages seven months to seventeen years old. I was curious about the seven month old. How many siblings would there be and what would be the chance it was a girl? Would her social worker even consider us as prospective parents? They had that power to say the baby wasn't the right ethnicity for us or that they didn't want to drive two hours to check up on her. If the baton-lady had any say, we probably had 0% chance.

I went to the bathroom to wash up for lunch just as the children started coming in. I saw a lady come in pushing a chubby baby in a stroller. I figured that must be the seven month old and it looked like the baby had no siblings.

We had pizza for lunch and the waiting children sat across from the prospective parents. There was a cute two year old with an attitude twice her size that caught our eye and after lunch we played with her a little. She was dark and wore cute little round glasses. She was really adorable and Pat was quite taken with her. She reminded me of Rafael. Rafael could wear a person out when he was that age. Terrible twos times two. I couldn't quite handle the thought of dealing with that attitude again so soon and she just wasn't the right "sand dollar."

There were so many children to play with so we tried to keep to the fifteen minute limit. One fifteen year old girl kind of confronted us and wanted to know what age of child we were looking for. She was not supposed to ask that kind of question, but she had a glint in her eye along with a look of despair that it was always the same; that fear that no one wanted her. I was promising myself never to go to one of those picnics again as I took another bathroom break while Pat went looking for another lonely child to play with.

He saw the seven month old then. The baby was with his social worker and his foster mom. Pat walked on trying to find me. Now he was for sure ready to take me home- before I saw the baby. He was pretty sure that once I saw this seven month old, he would have to give up his dream of having another little girl. He circled the building looking for me, but I had gone back out just after he had gone around the corner, so we missed each other.

That's when I found Mr. seven month old. It looked like no one was having their turn with him so I went to take a turn.

I met his foster mom, Frances. I could tell she cared deeply for this baby and his future. I liked her and his social worker instantly. Frances was happy to answer all my questions. Baby Dylan Jonathan Doe was seven months old but he held his body like a three month old. He had spina bifida and hydrocephalus. Frances asked if I wanted to hold him and had me sit down first until I got used to holding this twenty-three pound chunk. He wore a soft white shirt with some animal pictures on it and some little short pants. He had adorable little braces on his feet. He was so soft, so perfect, with the most heart-melting little smile. I never wanted to let go. And then Pat found me.

We had a million questions. Frances was honest with her answers. She and the social worker told us what the doctors said and what Frances saw, which were two different things. Frances said his body was delayed and he maybe would never walk. But he was just as smart as any seven month old baby even though the doctors said it wasn't possible. All I cared at that point was that he was in my arms. I whistled softly a little ways from his ear to see what he would do. He rewarded me with a sideways glance and a shy little smile. He was a charmer and I was completely charmed. I felt his soft hair. It was the softest hair. I felt down the right side of his head where his little shunt was. I wondered if it hurt him.

"No," Frances said, "it's like part of his body."

I couldn't believe I didn't mind all of these things. I was not afraid or freaked out or anything.

I stretched my fifteen minutes alarmingly past fifteen. There wasn't anybody asking to hold him, but I finally gave him up before I got the baton. I was ready to fill out the "interested" paper so we could see if we would be considered a match. Pat still teased me that maybe we should fill one out for the two year old girl, but he willingly helped me fill out our paper for the seven month old baby boy.

We came across Frances and baby Dylan again and another prospective mom was holding him. When she saw me she said, "Here, you can have him back," just as though he were mine already and she didn't want to take up our time together. I told her that she was welcome to hold him and she had just as much right to as I did. But she insisted on giving him to me. I hadn't even met her or noticed her before. How was she so sure he was mine? I knew I wore my heart on my sleeve, but seriously?

We finally pulled ourselves away and said our goodbyes. I think we were one of the last ones to leave. I wondered what would happen after that. How long would we wait before we got a call saying the social worker was ready to do a disclosure meeting with us? Or would we ever get the call? Would we be considered capable of caring for this special child? Would they think we had enough to offer him?

I was nauseated on the way home. My emotions had gone so many places in so little time. My head was in a whirl. Pat was worried we wouldn't know how to care for someone so special. I was worried, too, to tell the truth. It was too much to process. I thought my head would burst.

CHAPTER 9

When we got home the children wanted to know if we had found her. I knew the question was coming. Lissandra was especially waiting for her. At nine years old she was an intense little girl. Her feelings ran deep. Pat was very worried about her acceptance of a boy instead of the long dreamed-of girl. He was all Daddy-not-wanting-his-little-girl-unhappy. I prayed I would be able to tell her just how wonderful the little person we had met really was, so it would be easier for her to accept the change of plans.

We were fixing supper and she was asking me about our day. I told to her we had met a very special baby boy.

"Not a girl?"

"No, a very sweet little boy..."

She stopped setting the table. She looked out the window and I saw tears in her eyes. I was glad her daddy wasn't there to see. I nearly couldn't take it myself. How was she going to handle this? Would she break down and cry and question our judgment? I saw her put her hand on her hip. I waited. She turned to me and what she said nearly broke me completely.

She said, "Mommy, God must have a reason for this ... for us wanting a girl and giving us a boy instead."

Yes, I was sure He did. And silently I thanked God for putting such understanding in her little heart, because I sure couldn't explain it all.

At the supper table we talked about how cute baby Dylan was. That he was Hmong. The soft black hair he had and his winning smile and chubby cheeks. Oh! And he had the cutest slanty eyes and the prettiest brown skin. And when they saw his smile they would know why we fell in love and they were going to fall in love, too.

Their eyes sparkled. They were so anxious to hear all we could tell them. We answered all the questions as best we could. After supper and dishes were done, we sat in the living room. We talked about how big he was and could he walk already? No, he had a very special condition that meant he might not ever walk. He had spina bifida. He was born with a hole in his back that they had to sew up, so he had a big scar on that spot. And he wore little braces on his feet so he wouldn't get drop foot, because he had no muscle tone in his lower body.

Up until then, Marcio had been enthused and excited. He was my little show off, but underneath he had the softest biggest heart. So, his reaction to his new brother not walking surprised us. He said he would not have a brother that couldn't walk!

We were dumbfounded. I tried to see into his mind. I could hardly believe he had a prejudice against someone who couldn't walk. I was not prepared for this. He was nearly in tears and all our questions, trying to understand why that was a problem to him, seemed to just frustrate him. We told him he would not care once he saw him and held him.

Nope, he would have nothing of it.

I went to bed puzzling over it all. I was glad Rafael was young enough and that some of those things were not a big deal to him. But why was Marcio having such trouble with it? I tried to remember situations that we had been in where Marcio would have been with someone who had a disability. How had he acted or reacted? I could never recall him being mean or ever making fun of anyone. Rather, he had such deep empathy when he thought someone was in pain. Like the day my friend had come over to see me. When she came in, she flopped down on the couch to wait for me to finish what I was doing. Marcio, meanwhile, had asked her if he could get her a drink of water. I wondered at that, as she had not said she was thirsty. He got her a drink and they chatted. He seemed very solicitous. I was mystified. She was not sick that I could see. I sat down to visit and sent him off to play. In a bit, she was pouring her heart out to me. She had walked in my door with the world on her shoulders and Marcio's radar had picked up on pain, invisible to me, and had tried to soothe it the best way he knew. I had thought I was pretty keen at picking up on people's distress, especially my close friends. But my seven year old was certainly keener that day. To suffer when others suffer can be so painful.

Then why? Ahh! There was my answer. I knew then. He was afraid of his own emotional pain at seeing someone not able to get up and walk and run like he could. He was afraid he would not be able to handle it.

Once I knew where he was coming from, it was easier to know how to approach him. He remained adamant that he didn't want this baby. I knew in my heart that his heart would be won, but we had to give him time.

CHAPTER 10

We were in that state of nervous waiting. When would they call to set up a date to meet with us and ask all their questions? Would we be deemed good enough to be this baby's parents?

In less than a week we got the call. Our social worker wondered if we could be in San Jose for the disclosure meeting on Friday of the following week. That was quicker than we had anticipated! We went quaking in our boots. We were faced with more social workers in one setting than we had ever faced before. None of them seemed austere or scary, though, so we gathered a little courage. We were glad our social worker was there. Dylan's social worker (who was going on maternity leave) and her replacement were there along with the head social worker. We sat at a big oval table. Frances, the foster mom, was there also. I had really hoped baby Dylan would be there, but maybe they weren't sure enough about us yet to let us see him again so they hadn't brought him.

The social worker presenting Dylan's case began with introductions. Then she told Frances to tell us what she knew about Dylan. She was very passionate about this baby and about his well being. She showed us photos of him when he was in the hospital. Of his little back after they had finally sewed it shut after CPS had stepped in and said it had to be done. They had let him lay with it open, not closing it, thinking he would not live. They had waited seventy-two hours to put in a shunt to relieve his little head of its extra fluid. The neurosurgeon said the damage had been done because of too much pressure on the brain for so long. Frances told us that the neurosurgeon gave little hope of Dylan living. If he did, he would never develop properly, mentally or physically. For sure he would never walk. The doctor had made sure the birth mother had been told this also. She had not had the means to care for such a special child so she had walked away from the hospital and left him as a surrender baby.

Frances explained how his shunt drained the fluid in his head. The first shunt they put in had worked for a while and then at four months something was not right. He was fussing a lot so Frances took him in to see the neurosurgeon. They had to do surgery and put in a smaller size shunt because the one he had was making him over-drain, causing head pressure. He did well after that shunt revision and was again a happy, contented baby. She told us something could go wrong anytime and he had to be watched closely for changes.

Even Pat, who had been an EMT and enjoyed the medical world, was feeling inadequate and overwhelmed. Me, I didn't care for all things medical at all and was feeling like I would never be capable of caring for Dylan, even while I knew I would do anything for him. When Frances was done explaining the doctors' view of it all, we asked her to tell us what her gut feeling was about this baby. She was more than happy to, but made sure we knew it was her opinion and it wasn't at all like the doctors' opinions.

She felt he was ahead of his age cognitively. He was very alert and developing properly. His motor skills were delayed by at least four months. He was seven months old, but he held his body like a three month old. With therapy, he was making progress, but everything took great effort and was hard work for him. She believed one day he would be able to walk with some assistance. She could not say how long his new shunt would work. So many things played into the success of a shunt.

When she was done giving us her load of information, our minds were in serious overload. And we wondered if the social workers would start in with their warnings of the difficulties we would face and proceed to ask us the dreaded questions. But to our great surprise, the head social worker asked the others if they had anything to add and no one did. She turned to us and we braced ourselves, but she had only one question for us. "Do you have any questions?"

We could not believe our ears. And, no, we had no more questions. I didn't think I could handle one more drop of information. The only question I had, I was too scared to ask. I wanted to know when I could see and hold my baby again. I thought they would surely say something if we were supposed to see him. But no one said a word. Later Frances told me that they had expected us to ask and wondered why we didn't.

They told us they normally give parents forty-eight hours to decide if they wanted to proceed or not, but because we were going into the weekend, we would have a little more time. They would expect a call from us on Monday with our answer.

As we walked back to the parking garage, our social worker walked beside me. He had been very quiet throughout the meeting. I was curious what he thought, as he had not been at the picnic and had not seen baby Dylan or my attachment to him.

His answer surprised me. He said, "I knew from the moment you told me about meeting Dylan that you would take this baby."

What was he saying? He was so *sure.* He had helped place many children in his life, so he knew what to look for, but I still could not see how he knew.

I knew what my heart was saying, but I also knew that I only wanted God's answer. I also knew that, between me and Pat, I was the positive, move-ahead type. He had questions I overlooked in my eagerness to try a new challenge. This was a challenge we had to be sure was right for us. I knew I had the love, but did I have the wisdom? I knew that Pat had to make the final answer. We had to be together in this.

On Saturday, I did my usual work around the house, but my mind was miles away. My emotions were in a tumble. I told Pat that even though I had many questions I did not see how I could say no. I didn't think I would ever be able to live with myself if I did. I told him those were my feelings, and it was my heart, but I would not try to persuade him in any way.

Lissandra was very sure we should be calling as soon as we got up Monday morning and say "yes." She was dismayed that her daddy was not so sure. She told him that God would be there for us and she thought he just needed to trust God.

That night after the children were in bed, I read my Sunday School lesson for the next day. I do not recall what the topic was. As I read, I prayed that God would send an answer; something to calm my fears. I read hungrily for answers. Really, how was I to care for a child that needed so much special care? My three had never been hospitalized, had had very few mishaps; not even a broken bone. How would I know what to do?

My mind whirled, and as I read I came to a paragraph that talked about how the mothers had brought their babies to Jesus and had given them to Him so He could heal them. A quiet, calm assurance came over me. And in my heart I knew, "This is the same Jesus of long ago. When mothers did not know how to care for their hurting, sick children they placed them in Jesus' arms. He gave them answers. He will do the same for you! He knows everything this child will need."

Yes! This child was in God's hands. It wasn't my place to know it all. All I had to do was trust God and He would direct.

I did not tell Pat about my little message from God for two reasons. One, was because it was so special to me and I just wanted to hold that special moment close. I wanted to treasure it and "ponder it in my heart." The second reason was that Pat was not ready to hear it. Until he asked or said something that would tell me he was ready, I felt I would be trying to persuade him by telling him.

We went to church Sunday morning longing for God to speak to us. Pat told me on the way home that he had received some direction from God and he wondered if I had, too. I told him I had and that I felt more at ease, especially after I realized that we were not the ones in charge, but our Jesus was.

We talked about our fears and came to the same conclusion together. This child was God's. All our children were God's and only through Him could we even think of being parents at all. Jesus knew and understood what we didn't. Our answer was "Yes!"

CHAPTER 11

Monday morning! I was anxious to get the phone call to the social worker in, but I kept my mouth shut, amazingly. We had decided Pat would make the call and he needed to do it in his own time. I didn't have long to wait before I heard him call and say we would like to continue with the adoption of baby Dylan. We had played a long three year waiting game and I could hardly believe it was over.

Many phone calls followed and before I knew it the social workers had turned the transition planning over to Frances and me. We decided the best time to get together would be the following Thursday at her house in San Jose. Just Pat and I would go for the first visit to see Dylan. The children weren't too happy about that, especially Lissandra.

We decided to name our new son Alex Joseph. Joseph, because Pat's middle name is Joseph. Since he was a surrender baby, he had been named Dylan by the hospital staff. Jonathan Doe was tagged on because he was in essence a person with no home or family. Frances started by calling him Dylan Alex at first. Later we would change it to Alex Dylan and eventually drop the Dylan completely once he was familiar enough with the change.

I had some soft burp cloths from Brazil that my mom had given me. All my babies had had them for sleeping and cuddling. I left some with Frances for Alex so he could start becoming familiar with us. We drove to Frances' house on Thursday. Both his social workers were there for a short time just to make sure all went well.

There was no need to worry. Frances was a pro at making people feel comfortable and at ease. I don't think she knows a stranger. We also met her husband, Nathan, and their two teenage children, Smitty and Bridget. Smitty was definitely one of Alex's favorite people. He glowed with happiness when Smitty played with him and tossed him around. We were amazed at how they played together. We had kind of thought we had to be extra careful with Alex, but we soon found out he got normal treatment. Were we ever glad of that!

I held Alex all I could and we talked to him a lot so he would get used to us and our voices. Frances had me feed him his baby food and bottles and change his diapers. She told us the best way to hold him and what his favorite things were. He seemed to like me and not feel strange with me as I cuddled and talked to him.

Frances told us she wanted to be called Oma (Grandma) by Alex and my other three. Nathan would be Opa (Grandpa). She said that was what all her foster children called her. We liked the idea. It was respectful and warm all at the same time.
She told us to bring the children down to their farm by Selma on Saturday. We would go and spend the day. It was hard for me to leave my baby and go home even though it was for only a day, and I could hardly wait.

We pulled ourselves away and headed for home. We hit rush hour and decided to stop at a shopping mall to wait for the traffic to thin out. We went into a Barnes and Noble and browsed a while. I was delighted to find a treasure. I love the *Chicken Soup* for the Soul books and found a copy of *Chicken Soup for the Special Needs Soul.* I also got *One Tattered Angel.* It is a heart warming book about a very special child a family adopted. I had talked to Frances about it and she had said she wanted to read it. I decided to give one to her by way of a token of thanks for taking care of Alex for us until we could. I would wait to give it to her when we had the dedication for Alex she had planned at her friend Pattie's.

We faced innumerable questions when we got home. The children could hardly wait until Saturday. When the day came, I was a bundle of nerves on the way to the farm. I tried to relax and breathe deep. I don't think I was nervous about any particular thing; I just had too many thoughts whirling through my head and so many emotions!

We found their farm house nestled in a vineyard. They had brought Frances' grandma along for the weekend so we got to meet her and Frances' dad who lived on the farm.

Marcio and Rafael said a quick hello to Alex and then they were glued to Smitty. He had a small motorcycle and gave them rides. He liked kids, which was definitely a plus, seeing as he had two leeches to deal with all day.

Lissandra was glued to my side trying to make friends with Alex. He wasn't as eager to bond as she was. His world had consisted of adults and not children, so he wanted his space. But Lissandra was totally smitten whether Alex agreed to it or not.

It was just so wonderful to hold him again and cuddle with him. I gave him up only for Lissandra to hold him or for his nap. Pat talked to him, but was never one to enjoy holding babies before they were a year or older. He let me do the bonding. He would have his chance later. He hit it off with Nathan and they walked around the farm and talked. We had a very relaxing day together. Later, Frances told me that Grandma had wondered if I would ever put that poor baby down. That made me smile. Not if I could help it, I wouldn't.

I asked questions about Alex's care. Frances knew so much and I felt like I was starting at ground zero. If Frances had disappeared out of my life at that point, I would have gone into a legitimate, full-blown panic attack. But I had her and she was my Alex-encyclopedia. I was amazed how much I loved her so soon. She seemed like a sister that had been hidden away and had appeared all of a sudden, ready to sister me along. I thanked God for having given Alex such a wonderful person as a foster mom. She and Nathan had had to make the decision whether to adopt Alex themselves or not. Through much praying for God's direction in this, the answer came clearly that they needed to pursue placing him in another home — a Christian home, they prayed.

The wonder of God's perfect plan for our lives seemed to be before us like a beautiful scene. Those long years of waiting and agonizing seemed to have just been a blanket over the canvas. We knew it was there, waiting to be revealed ... well, most of the time we did. I had to remember how I had been inspired to pray with such earnestness the January before. Those prayers had been answered and the scene before me was all the more colorful and exquisite because of the tears that had accompanied it. I was awestruck. The joy was so complete. I had not expected to feel so full of happiness and joy. It was like heaven in my soul. It made my heart sing the song of those that wait upon the Lord. All that time, God had been mixing the colors and painting. Each stroke had meaning, a purpose. Each prayer had been heard and used in making the most beautiful hues. His ways are perfect!

Frances taught us all a little song she had made up while Alex was still in the hospital. She said she really couldn't sing. And we could attest to this being true, bless her heart. But it only made this little song all the more amazing because it was so perfect. It was a soothing tune and she sang it to Alex often. It touched me deeply. The words were so full of entreaty; I believe God heard it every time it was sung and healed Alex in some little way:

"Jesus, heal my little head; Jesus, heal my little head, so I can be a thinking man of God.

Jesus, heal my little legs; Jesus heal my little legs, so I can be a standing man of God.

Jesus, heal my little feet; Jesus, heal my little feet, so I can be a walking man of God."

CHAPTER 12

Our next visit was in San Jose again. Frances took us along to Alex's therapy appointment so we could discuss his future goals with the therapist. We learned a lot, but it was overwhelming. I was glad they videoed the things they were trying to teach him so I could see it again later and learn how to work with him under less pressure.

They were working on teaching him to roll over. For Alex, that meant months of teaching and helping him build enough muscle to do this simple task on his own. He was content to lie on his back and play, so he did not exactly appreciate our efforts to get him out of his comfort zone. This is very common for children with spina bifida. It was mom and the therapist that had to be the cheer leaders, motivators, and action pushers.

I was glad that the therapist understood what to do and when to do it to help him develop because I sure had no clue. I was ready to drive to San Jose each week to get him good therapy. I had been told that our county was the worst in California for getting services because they had such a huge caseload. I was concerned I wouldn't get Alex into therapy quickly enough or find a good therapist, but Alex's therapist told us she thought it would be best to find him therapy close to home, even if it meant a little wait. It was good advice, but at the time I was feeling so insecure, I could hardly see the wisdom in it.

The next few weeks were filled with visits to San Jose. We went to see Alex's primary care doctor and get all his records. We had to go see his neurosurgeon and he ordered some scans and sent many records on CDs with us. We went to his urologist and he did some tests. We had to go to the hospital for the scans. It was an upper scale hospital. We felt out of our league, but there was an air of competence that made us feel like we were in good hands. And the valet parking with drivers that wore spotless white shirts and black ties made us feel some kind of snazzy.

When we decided it was time for Alex to spend a night at our house, we went to San Jose to get him. We left the children with friends and went on a Friday night when Nathan and Frances were going out of town for the weekend, so we had their house to ourselves. We had a lovely time just relaxing and enjoying our quiet time with Alex in his familiar surroundings. Saturday morning, we had breakfast, packed up the diaper bag, and headed home with Alex.

Oh! It was so inexpressibly wonderful to take our baby home, even if it was for a short visit. He was so good about it all, although he cried inconsolably when we were going through the hills. We did not know if the change in elevation caused head pressure or if he suddenly felt he was in a very strange place. But he hated going through hills with a passion for years after that.

On Sunday morning, it was so exciting to take Alex to church for the first time and show him off to my friends. They thought he was so cute ... but would he grow into his head? His head was a couple sizes too big for his body because of his hydrocephalus and it was something that took people back at first. Then his charming smile made them forget all about it. He calmly took in all the attention and his new surroundings.

Nathan and Frances came to get Alex Sunday afternoon. Lissandra did not understand transitioning was easier for the baby even if it was hard on the rest of us, and was not looking forward to Alex leaving. Nathan and Frances stayed all afternoon and went to church with us in the evening. When they packed up and we had to say goodbye, Lissandra was heartbroken. Her little brother belonged with her, not miles away. Frances was near tears just watching her and decided it would be best to speed up the transition. So, instead of having several short overnight stays like we had planned, the next time we went to see Alex, the whole family went along and we brought him home to stay.

We went that week to get our black haired little man with the sweet smile. On the way home we stopped to eat lunch. We tried to act normal, but our excitement must have shown because it seemed like people just stared at us. We weren't in the mood to mind. I felt like staring at our baby myself.

A couple weeks later, Frances had a dedication service for Alex at her friend, Patty's. It was a beautiful time of dedicating Alex's life into God's hands as he became part of our family. A youth pastor, who was a friend of Bridget's, performed the ceremony. When he asked me and Pat to share how God had led us to Alex, Pat, who is the less emotional of us two, began to cry as he told of our journey to Alex and the joy he had brought us already. I don't think anyone had a dry eye in the room. I had so much in my heart, but so few words to express it. It was such a beautiful day and it helped Frances with letting go. Nathan and Frances would definitely be a part of our lives and they wanted our children to call them Oma and Opa like all her foster kids did after they were placed. She gleefully played grandma to them, then let us repair the damage at home. One way to get grandkids, I guess.

Meanwhile, we were feeling so fulfilled. My arms were so wonderfully filled and our family felt so complete. We had not expected so much joy. We decided we definitely wanted to experience it again ... down the road a ways.

CHAPTER 13

We began the task of transferring Alex's records to our county. We were assigned a neurosurgeon at the Children's Hospital in Fresno. Fresno was an hour drive for us, give or take depending on traffic.

We were a bit apprehensive about new doctors and a new hospital. Would they be as good as what Alex had before? We felt so vulnerable and naive. Would we be able to get him all the care he needed? Only the comfort of Jesus' promise that He would direct us and tell us what to do kept us calm and able to take one thing at a time. We were so thankful we had Frances and the social workers to help us through the maze.

When we went for Alex's first appointment at the Children's Hospital and for some tests and x-rays, it was a cloudy, gray day. We drove down a two-lane road out in farm country past citrus orchards and fields after we got off the freeway. It just wasn't your normal drive to a hospital and we wondered if we had taken the wrong road. Then we came around a bend and there it was! The hospital was situated out in the country, up on a bluff overlooking the valley and the river. On the other side of that narrow valley was Fresno. It was a beautiful location. The hospital grounds had acres of green lawn with trees in the back. The sidewalks were lined with flowers. In the front there were shrubs trimmed into animal shapes. By the front door they were shaped into tall giraffes. The hospital's mascot was a giraffe named George.

Inside, the walls were colorful and full of floor-to-ceiling animal scenes. The cafeteria walls were painted like the bottom of the ocean. It was the most amazing hospital I had ever been to.

In spite of being well-cared for, we kept searching for that air of business-like competence we had felt at the other hospital. It was so relaxed and had such an at-home feeling, it made us wonder if we would get proper care. Then, suddenly it hit me! The hospital in San Jose had been like riding in a limousine. This hospital was like riding in a VW beetle. Both got you to your destination and that was what mattered. Come to think of it, the beetle was definitely more down our line. How long could simple folk like us have enjoyed a limo ride anyway?

Alex had only had one shunt replacement at the age of four months. All had gone well after that and I convinced myself that it would likely just continue on that way. I mean, who wants their smooth ride to end? I would not let myself think of Alex having any serious complications. I could not bear the thought of Alex's shunt going bad and needing to go in for surgery. We had so many adjustments that I do not think I would have coped so well with an emergency run to the hospital during those first months, and God graciously spared us from that.

We had plenty to do. A teacher came to our home once a week to play with Alex and make sure he was developing properly. She was a sweet, grandmotherly lady who had years of experience teaching children with special needs. She was very good at what she did. There was only one problem:
Alex didn't like her.

We soon learned Alex disliked people when they were too eager to make friends with him. Most people do this with the best intentions, but Alex hated the focus being on him. He would crawl into his little shell when he felt overwhelmed. He much sooner made friends if people would wait and he could make the first move. Well, Miss Doreen was being the best teacher she knew to be. She would make her bold approaches and Alex would clam up and be the best little snappy turtle in a shell he could be. It was a bit stressful to watch her have to push and shove to get a response out of him. He was plainly irritated with her. I was helpless to know how to help. You can't force someone to like someone else. She had a British accent, and she said the only words she couldn't say like the rest of us were, "bononuh" (banana) and "wotuh" (water).
I can't say we completely agreed with her.

She tried to teach Alex basic sign language. If he was done playing with a toy and wanted another one, he had to make the sign for "mohh" (more). Every week, she tried to get him to do this and every week she had to pick up his hands and help him do it. I was not sure if he was actually not catching on or if he was just plain refusing to do it. He was starting to say quite a few words so I was a bit puzzled. One evening at supper, he wanted more food. He looked at me sweetly and made the the sign for "more" at the same time saying, "mohh."

He was playing games with his teacher! Acting dumb, so he didn't have to perform. Needless to say, we had us some secret chuckles over his impertinence.

Alex was stubborn for her, but he was doing so well that she finally said she was not teaching him anything. Her job was to help children get caught up to their age level. Alex was doing things ahead of his age level, so she did not think he needed her any more. I was happy for one less appointment each week. Alex ... let's just say he was happy too.

We had periodic visits from Alex's social worker in San Jose. The first time she was supposed to come, I was hurrying around making sure everything was in perfect order. I was cleaning up the bathroom and had Alex playing in his high chair in the kitchen. Sandy and Marcio were at school. Rafael was playing in the kitchen by Alex. Suddenly, I heard a kind of scream from Alex and Rafael hollered in a desperate voice. I ran into the kitchen just in time to see Rafael take his hands off of Alex's shoulders. Alex was bleeding at the mouth. I asked Raf what was happening. He said Alex had been leaning over biting his tray, as he had a habit of doing.

I have to insert here that Alex had gotten both of his two top front teeth and his two bottom ones in. His perfect little toothy smile was a source of great pride to me. Well, a fourth of my pride was laying sideways in Alex's mouth. When he was biting the edge of his tray, his bottom teeth got caught. When he went to raise his head, he couldn't, so he screamed. Rafael was trying to help him get free and it jarred his tooth loose. Well, it was more than loose. It was lying sideways and came right out when I tried to straighten it. I was so dismayed. I did not know that the loss of my baby's tooth could make me so sad. He would only grow another one to fill the space when he was five or six years old.

What was I going to tell his social worker? She came a few minutes later and she felt bad for Alex, but was unconcerned otherwise. She had three boys of her own. She knew what it was like. Things happen.

Whew! I could breathe again.

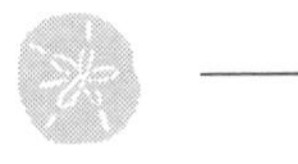

CHAPTER 14

Christmas was extra special for us that year. Having our baby boy to hold turned my thoughts often to the joy Mary must have felt when she held her Baby Boy.

My grandpa passed away that December and my dad came up to Kansas from Brazil for Grandpa's funeral. We were not able to go because of some job commitments Pat had made. But we were able to spend Christmas with my dad. It was the first time my dad saw any of our boys. I think it had been eight years since I had seen him.

We made the proper arrangements for Alex to leave the state with us. Pat's parents and sisters were in Kansas to spend Christmas with Pat's grandpas. So, we all spent Christmas day together.

Pat's younger sister, Beth, and her husband had adopted their son from Guatemala. It was a special time for us all, to have Alex and their son, Ramon, together for their first Christmas. Their Grandma and Great Grandma sure were proud of them. We wished my mom could have been there to enjoy Alex's first Christmas too.

Alex was a good traveler except for a few surprises. On the way to Kansas he suddenly threw up all over. We knew that could be a symptom of a shunt malfunction and that made us worry a bit. We watched him really close after that. He didn't throw up again during our drive to Kansas so we relaxed our strict vigil a bit. Then, halfway through our stay he got a fever, which lasted a couple days. We kept a close watch again, but it appeared to be the flu. He also had a bout of naughtiness in which he was very difficult and produced an all-out tantrum a time or two. Only he did not kick like most eleven month olds would. He just screamed and would turn his head away when we talked to him. He had some spirit, that was for sure. Though the tantrums were not so pleasant to work through, I was glad he had that kind of fight in him. If we could channel it in the right direction, it would help him through life. It would take wisdom and patience. God said He would be there to help me care for this child, so I was counting on it.

When we got home from our trip to Kansas, Alex was just delighted to be back home where he could roll around on the floor and play with his toys.

He was doing well with sitting, but was not able to get from lying down to a sitting position by himself. He worked hard at it because it was something he wanted to master. Things sure went better when it was his idea to do something new.

One day he amazed us by telling his sister, "Num, num, peash," when he wanted some of her ice cream. We, of course, thought he was the smartest kid on the planet. I mean, that was almost a sentence and he was not a year old yet. Alex was also a smoocher. He gave big slobbery kisses and his sister was always begging for one. Sometimes, he got so fed up with her begging, he applied teeth to try and teach her a lesson. She became more careful about asking for kisses from that little mister.

On the 22nd of January he was a year old; one year longer than the doctors had thought he would live. We were mighty glad they had been wrong. And the day after his birthday, Rafael started kindergarten. That meant no playmate three days a week for Alex.

On the 24th of January we had an appointment at the Spina Bifida Clinic. There we would meet his new doctors, nutritionist, psychologist, and social worker. This team would ensure Alex got all the care he needed. We were nervous about it, but excited at the same time. We had to go early and do a couple more tests at the hospital, which was on the same grounds as the clinic. That made for a long day for us. When we got to the clinic, they put us in an exam room. We would be there until every team member had been in to see us. We had Frances come with us so she could help us with the transition. I wondered if I would ever be able to handle the medical issues without her.

The head nurse came first and we loved her. She would be the person we would call on many times to help us find answers. She was one of those angels who walked into your lives and made the burdens of life much lighter.

We met the urologist, who said all looked good. Alex had a neurogenic bladder, but testing showed it to be working properly. Someday we would need to catheterize him. They had us watch a video and gave us a kit to take home to do a test to see if it would benefit him to start cathing right away. We were not ready for this and we were very glad when the results showed that it was not necessary yet. Until the age of five he would be more prone to infections and catheterizing sooner than that would only increase the risk. A bladder infection, if it got bad enough, could follow the catheter that drained from his head into his abdomen, back up to his shunt. That was enough to scare me. We were warned to watch for fevers. A fever for Alex was not to be ignored!

When the orthopedic doctor came in he told us Alex probably would never walk and left as soon as he was done with the examination. We had so many questions we wanted to ask, but he barely answered the few we had the courage to ask because of his brusque manner. It upset us a bit, and Frances even more. Whether Alex walked or not, only time would tell, but to be told so by someone who had never seen our child before was not so easy to take. It was true that in the eyes of a doctor it appears a certain way because of all he has seen, but a doctor had once said Alex would not live and if he did, he would "never be anything in society." Alex was daily proving him wrong and that kind of talk simply would not deter us from helping Alex thrive.

The nutritionist drove me crazy. Why they try telling a mother that her perfectly healthy child needs to change his diet is beyond me. Now, if what that child is eating is causing the child to have a bad immune system or making them obese, or fail to thrive, then I certainly would want their expert advice. In all our spina bifida clinics in the years to come, the nutritionist was my least favorite visitor. I know they are trained for this and it's their job. I get it. Sometimes their agony over my not doing exactly what the books say to do was actually kind of comical, but annoying just the same.

The therapist was very helpful and gave us some good tips. The social worker was there to make sure Alex was getting all the services he was entitled to. She would intercede if we had any trouble with any member of the team or any trouble at the hospital and needed help getting services. We rarely called upon the social worker in the coming years, but it was a comfort to know she was there.

Our most favorite was Alex's neurosurgeon. She was an energetic lady that looked much younger than she said she was and we liked her immensely. She wasn't a know-it-all and told us doctors do not have all the answers to hydrocephalus. They do what they know to do and, as each person is made differently, the answers are not always the same. She said the parents were definitely the ones who knew the child best and what they said carried a lot of weight with her. In the coming years, she lived up to that, too. I was happy to see that Frances was as pleased with her as we were.

Little did any of us know how very well we would get to know this fun, energetic lady.

CHAPTER 15

In February, my parents came to see us. Excitement ran high. They stayed a week or so with us. Alex sure loved his Grandma Becker and I was glad he did. I had been a bit worried he wouldn't as he was very stand-offish to his Grammy Baize, who did everything she could to win him over. He was just quicker to like a person if they waited for him to make the first move. And that was probably why he had a hard time with Lissandra, or Sandi, as we came to call her. She tried so hard to win his love. We finally told her she needed to step back and let Alex ask for her. This brought a few tears, but things went a little better between them after that.

Pat's mom was not pushy, but she treated Alex with the same affection she had her other grandchildren. Alex had his own set of rules and she must have crossed a line in his mind. My mom must have been just a bit less demonstrative and that seemed to make the difference. He was sure a silly little guy.

A month or two after Alex turned one, I decided to count all the words he could say. I counted at least twenty-five. I have to admit, I certainly would have loved to show that list to those smart medical people that said he would never be anything but a burden to society, "and never amount to anything." His words were clear and easy to understand. One of his first words was "Dadda." He dearly loved his Daddy, and when Pat would get home from work, Alex would start calling for him to come see what he was playing. He would get a bit persistent and finally Daddy would answer in a teasing voice, " I'm busyyy!" or, "Can't you see I'm busy?"

Alex would giggle and call even more persistently. One day it backfired on Daddy, though. He called Alex and got his own medicine.

A little voice answered, "I'm busyyy!"

Alex's hatred for going through the hills continued. He would often cry or fuss until we were through them. As he got older, the fussing would begin when he saw hills ahead and he would beg us not to go through them. We just never knew what it was that bothered him so much about them.

One day we were on our way home from a not-so-pleasant stay up in the hills at a doctor's house we were good friends with. Alex had grumped and fussed most of the time there and we were ready to get him home. He was crying and screaming as we drove when suddenly he saw his most favorite thing coming down the road toward us. He had a passion for motorcycles and usually had a toy motorcycle in his hand wherever he went. He quit screaming when he saw three of them heading our way and said all in one breath, "Cycle, cycle, cycle!"

And then he went back to screaming.

He had this silly habit of closing his eyelids most of the way and then he would kind of wiggle them and try to peer out of the slits. It made him look strange indeed. You knew he was in a very ornery mood when he did this, or that he was pleasantly trying to evade orders.

He loved to sit by the hour and look at books and was very gentle with them. I don't think he ever tore a book or magazine intentionally. He would use them as song books and would sing away.

He started physical therapy and how he loved it! He loved Mr. Joe, the therapist, and would say when we were a block or two away yet, "Joe! Ball."

The therapist ordered a stander with wheels for Alex. In less than two minutes, he figured out how to run the stander they put him in to get him fitted. He loved trucks and he was thrilled to be in his own; "Brroom, brroom!" He was not happy at all when we took him out of the stander to put him in his stroller.

His therapist worked on trying to teach him to crawl. It took months of strengthening his muscles to get him to stay up on his hands and knees. His head was still too big for his body, so it was somewhat painful for him. He had to build strength so he could hold his head up and not dive forward. He was so content to just roll over on his back or his side and lay there playing with his toys. That was his favorite position for playing, even though he had finally mastered the lying-to-sitting trick. When he really wanted to go someplace he "snaked" his way there, using his forearms and elbows to pull himself along.

He spent as much time outside as he possibly could. He really couldn't get around too well, but he loved playing out there. I took to putting overalls on him all the time. Otherwise, with all his tummy scooting, he was soon pantless. I especially liked overalls because they hid the scar on his back. I didn't mind showing people his scar if they wanted to see it, but I didn't like to set Alex up for unexpected rude stares and thoughtless comments. And, on top of it all, he was so very cute in overalls. I think, besides having the smartest kid, we were pretty sure we had the cutest one too.

CHAPTER 16

One day while I was reading my Bible and praying, a very quiet message came to me. It was simple and straight forward. "You need to prepare your mind that Alex could need surgery." I felt perfect calm. It did not make me anxious. I just needed to prepare my mind to the possibility.

Alex had become a bit more irritable and for sure got grumpy when his bottle got taken away. I just chalked it up as adjustment pains. He was especially feisty toward Lissandra. Marcio just about could do no wrong in his eyes, though. Marcio and Rafael had invented this insanely loud, wild game of fall-on-the-pillows. Somehow they would send him flying onto a pile of pillows from off the bed. Shrieks of laughter would come from their room. I was sure screams of pain would come next and if I would tell them to please be more careful, they would assure me they were being as careful as could be. Or they would lay him on they back of the couch and he would tumble down onto the cushions. All I could think of was his legs getting twisted under him and breaking, but the boys simply were sure that Alex was immune to such. And the miracle is that he never did break anything.

One day, I looked out the utility window into the backyard to check on the boys. They weren't in the yard where they usually played. Something caught my eye further out and I saw them over on the field road, riding a bike down a steep little slope. Marcio and Rafael liked to fly down this hill on their little bikes and would do some ramping. Boys will be boys — I had no problem with that — except that this time there was an extra person seated in front of Marcio as he sailed down the hill on the itty bitty little bike seat built for one. My heart crept closer to my throat. I wondered when Alex's feet would go flying forward into the spokes, as he had no way of controlling them. I heard screams of sheer delight. It made me so happy to see Alex having some normal boy fun, even though it really was a dangerous thing for them to be doing. I didn't want to dampen their spirits and make them feel bad for giving their brother a ride, so I decided to call them in and not say anything about it until later. Then I would explain the danger to them and tell them they needed to find a less dangerous game to play.

Well, I forgot to say anything to them "later." So the next time it happened was when Oma and Opa were over to see us. We heard shrieks of laughter so we went to see what was happening and there they were sailing down the hill, with Alex shrieking and laughing and begging to go faster. Oma and Opa were soon laughing and applauding between tears of joy at seeing Alex so well adjusted and happy.

Not too long later, we went to Oma and Opa's farewell party in San Jose. They were headed for Africa to live by Frances's sister. Only God knew how hard it was for me to let my Alex dictionary/ encyclopedia and my moral support fly off to Africa. I would have to sprout my own wings and I was not looking forward to losing my cocoon.

CHAPTER 17

Alex's adoption day was set for May 12th. On the 7th, he was feverish and not at all happy. He had only had a fever once or twice before and I was still worried that a fever could mean a possible infection by his shunt. Later, we would realized that those infections usually happen shortly after a shunt revision, but I wanted to keep a close eye on Alex, so I had him in bed beside me. He was restless and kept kicking his feet up by his head, a habit he had when his head hurt. I got a foot in my face more than once. Or he would sit up and flop forward and sleep with his head down between his feet. I laid my ear up against his head as I snuggled him close, trying to help him relax and get comfortable. His cheek felt hot against mine ... and then I did a double take. I thought I surely was imagining things! I drew my ear away, then back against his head again.

I was not imagining! Alex's shunt was making a high pitched squeal! It was like the squeal of a faucet when you barely turn it on.

I suddenly remembered the quiet warning I had gotten from God a month or two before:

"Prepare your mind that Alex could need surgery."

I knew without a doubt that the time had arrived. I woke Pat up and we discussed what to do. While Alex was restless, he wasn't screaming in pain or in any apparent danger so we decided to wait until morning to call his neurosurgeon.

She told us to come to the Children's Hospital ER. He seemed to be feeling better, but his shunt was still zinging. We headed down and faced ER for the first time. It didn't take long for Alex to be known as the kid with the squeaky shunt. The nurses and doctors said they had never heard a shunt make that squealing sound. It didn't look like Alex had any plans of giving us a boring ride.

Alex was a trooper in the ER. He almost acted too good, like there was nothing wrong. He was sitting on my lap waiting for the doctor to come in and he told me, "I wuv you, Mommy." Then he got embarrassed and quickly acted like he hadn't said anything. Ah, but I had heard and my mama heart nearly burst with the joy it gave me. It was the first time he had said it so clear and used my name. It has been said that when you fall in love, you love so much it hurts. Truly. My heart ached with the love I felt for this child. I could hardly stand the thought of the process he would have to through before he would feel better.

When we saw his neurosurgeon we explained that if it wasn't an emergency we would like to wait for surgery until after the adoption for two reasons. One, we didn't want to be stuck at the hospital on that special day. Second, we didn't want the confusion of having to change his name on all the hospital paperwork after his name was legally Alex. If we waited until after the adoption there would be so much less confusion.

His doctor checked his CAT scan and x-ray results and said his shunt was still working, but it seemed to be partially blocked and that would require surgery to correct the problem. She would have to take out the old shunt and put in a new one. As for his fever, he must have had a slight flu, because a regular shunt malfunction does not usually bring on a fever. I wondered if it was just God's little way of helping us see something was wrong. She said the surgery could wait until after the 12th, so we agreed to bring him back in for surgery on the 15th.

CHAPTER 18

Adoption Day! We dressed Alex up in his new set of clothes and we all put on our best for this special day. He loved dressing up and caught our excitement. I prayed Alex would feel OK and be able to enjoy the day along with us. We had waited for so long for this moment! If joy could be measured with a gauge, ours would have been caught speeding.

All the adoption paperwork had been excessive, of course, but fairly easy. Alex was a surrender baby, so there had been no visits with his biological family. It was nice to have that little perk after all our worrying and waiting during the three years before we found Alex.

It had been six months since the day Alex had come to our home before the adoption was finalized. The waiting was over! The six months had just flown by. We were ready for this new chapter of our lives to begin. The day was all we could have ever wished it to be. It seemed like God had picked his finest angels and disguised them as humans, and gave them the task of making sure Alex had a beautiful adoption. We missed the dearest angels of all, though — Opa Nathan and Oma Frances, who were way over in Tanzania. But Smitty and Bridget were there and we were so glad they were. Alex was very happy to see Smitty again, though they scarcely had any time together, thanks to some social workers that kept the poor child bouncing from one set of arms to another.

We thought it was so special that the judge had a formal paper for us to sign, vowing that we were committed to taking care of Alex and loving him. It was not a legal document, just a special addition to the ceremony. It was so thoughtful and warm and was the crowning moment of the day. Signing the legal documents that Alex Joseph Baize was now our son was special, but somehow, that paper went to the heart of why we were there.

There were tears of joy and of awe. Awe at the presence of God and His beautiful way of bringing Alex into our lives. Someone said the words again that we had heard so many times before, when we told them how Alex came into our lives: "It was meant to be!"

Because our God prepared for us this child and we knew this definitely was meant to be. Only He could take a child that was diagnosed with certain death, or at best a miserable existence, and bless him with life, a healthy mind, and a will to live. Then at just the right moment He placed in our waiting arms this little treasure, with a smile that wrapped itself around our hearts and made us family.

CHAPTER 19

May 15, 2008 we headed for the Children's Hospital by Madera. We got Alex checked in and headed up to the surgical floor. He was fasting, of course, so we were too. We would go eat at the cafeteria while he was in surgery. Pat went and got food for us while I stayed in the second waiting room where parents could eat and rest while their child was in surgery. It was our first time so we were nervous and wanted to be near in case they needed us for anything. I ate my food in anxious haste. Dr. W. had said it would take an hour or so.

I was having a hard time with my emotions, but it wasn't that I was afraid. I knew God was in control and we trusted the neurosurgeon, but I had not anticipated the terror Alex felt when he was taken from us at the surgical room door. We gave our hugs and kisses and we heard him scream even after the big double doors closed behind them. He screamed until they placed the gas mask over his mouth and nose and, thankfully, within seconds he was asleep. Not even a minute went by from the time he was in my arms until he was asleep. But those few seconds of terror would affect him for years. They had given Alex some sweet pink stuff (verced) that was supposed to help him get groggy and unaware of what was actually happening. They said he wouldn't remember anything even though he was awake. We were naïve enough to believe it. It may have worked for other kids, but after a few surgeries we realized it wasn't taking away the pain of separation for Alex. He remembered all too well.

We even got suspicious that Alex's subconscious was not asleep during surgery. He became terrified of his bath. He went from a fearless happy swimmer to utter terror at being in any water. We suspected there had been a sound like water flowing that penetrated his subconscious.

We were overjoyed to see his surgeon and hear that all had gone well. She had replaced his old shunt with one that could be programmed without surgery, using a device with a strong magnet. That sounded like a good thing to us, to be able to control how much cerebral fluid went through his shunt, all without invasive surgery. Or was it? Only time would tell.

They had Radio Flyer wagons at the hospital for small children to ride in. As soon as Alex was feeling up to it, we loaded him up in the wagon with pillows and put on his little cloth hat that I had got for him especially for after surgery, and we walked the halls.

It took me a long time to not feel lost most of the time. But we figured it out and spent hours out on the beautiful lawn, or by the play ground. There was an extra special spot we loved to go to. It was at the back of the hospital on the edge of the property. There was an iron horse that was a memorial of some kind. Alex liked me to take him out of the wagon and set him on the horse. We had the view of the river from there and, to Alex's great joy, a full view of the helipad where he could watch Air George come and go. Just about nothing in this world could make Alex happier than watching helicopters and airplanes in action. Well, and motorcycles.

Alex's first stay at the Children's Hospital was only two days. It was so good to be back home. Alex was excited to be on the floor with his own toys again and see the chickies and the kitties. We were so new at all of this surgery stuff that we were very cautious about him doing too much too soon. We were thankful it was all over and Alex could start feeling better.

Pat taught Alex to make a "kkkk" sound as he made a cutting motion on his head when we would ask, "What did Dr. W. do to you?" One day Alex got ornery and patted his daddy's head and said, "Dr. kkkk."

On the fourth day at home we knew something was not right. Alex seemed to be having headaches. He felt best lying on his side with his head on the floor instead of sitting up to play. He was cranky and very hard to please. We called the doctor to see if she had suggestions for how to help him feel better. She said to bring him back in. To our great relief, it was only a UTI this time. It was his first UTI and not something to mess around with so they kept him at the hospital for a couple of days to make sure he was going to be OK.

We went home, hopeful that our little bumps in the road were smoothing out and life would soon be back as it should be.

CHAPTER 20

We had one lovely month away from the hospital. Well, mostly lovely. Alex was not really feeling well and getting better after surgery like we had hoped he would. His irritability was high at times. We were learning that this meant he had too high of pressure in his little head or too low of pressure. On the 16th of June, we headed back to the hospital. Alex was admitted and he had scans and an MRI done. His doctor wanted to establish a "normal" for Alex. If we had a "normal" to work off of, she could compare scans. But thus far all the scans had shown him with swollen ventricles, so it was hard to determine exactly what was not working properly. Changing the shunt settings was not bringing lasting relief. Thankfully, she was not one to let it rest until she had it figured out.

On the 19th, Alex had a different size shunt put in, in hopes that it would help ease his head pressure. He was doing well, so Dr. W. ordered another MRI to see how his ventricles compared to before surgery. They definitely were smaller and he was happy. We were overjoyed when she said we could go home on the 23rd.

The Fourth of July came and so did Alex's mobile stander. He got to wheel around with the children at the park and he loved it. Some of his little friends cried, though, because they wanted a stander to ride in too!

Pat's sister Jill and her family came to visit from South Dakota. Aunt Jill fell in love with Alex and they had a lot of fun together and did a bit of rough housing. Very mild rough housing, but some jostling around, just the same. We soon noticed that the area by Alex's shunt was filling up with fluid just under the skin. I felt around by his shunt and something felt loose. Pat checked, too, and we were both sure the catheter draining from his head had disconnected from where it hooks up to the catheter that went down his neck and on down into his abdomen. Jill felt terrible about it. She was sure she must have bumped it loose. Pat enjoyed teasing her about it, but we knew that something else had to have been the cause. Shunts just aren't that fragile or easy to mess up. We called the on-call NP. She would relay the message, "that the Baizes think son's shunt catheter has become disconnected."

The response was: "Not possible. That just doesn't happen."

We smirked. We knew. Alex had quickly become famous for doing and having symptoms that were "impossible," or strange, or just not in the books.

Dr. W. usually didn't disregard what we said, so we bided our time and waited for her to get back to us with a solution. Alex, meanwhile, did not seem to be in any pain, so we were in no hurry. We knew it meant surgery to fix it and we were glad for every day at home.

On the 17th of July, Alex had a scan done. Sure enough, it was as disconnected as could be. Pat had some fun teasing Dr. W. that she had said it couldn't happen and here on the x-ray was proof it did happen. She loved the banter. After surgery, she said when she had opened it all back up, she saw that she had failed to stitch it down the time before. Operator error! The fact that she owned up to it and didn't try to blame someone else made us trust her all the more.

Alex was spacing his shunt revisions out to a monthly occurrence. It was a difficult time for the older kids, but they had Grandpa and Grammy to help out. Pat would bring them down as often as possible to see us at the hospital. He took the biggest part of the load, making sure they had clean clothes and getting them to bed and fed in the morning. All this while trying to keep up with his work schedule. He would usually take them to his mom's for the day or to school, and then take them back home for the night.

Alex began understanding more and more when we headed down toward the hospital what he would have to face. Those trips were hard on us all. I would reach back and hold Alex's hand to comfort him and it always helped calm him down. He got to where he would ask, "Hold hand?"

It worked fine when Pat was driving, but not so well when I had to take Alex by myself. I would get a kink in my neck from reaching back while I drove. His car seat was in the middle so I could reach him, but it still put my arm at a bad angle. I would sing sometimes to try to distract him, always hoping he would fall asleep. The pressure in his head combined with his anxiety a lot of times made him very irritable and inconsolable. He could scream for miles on end. It was almost impossible to reason with him during those times. Sometimes, the pressure made him sleepy and he would sleep for short periods. I was so thankful for those little breaks. It is truly agonizing for a mother to watch her child suffer and have so little she can do. I prayed to the Healer many times as we took that hour long trek to the hospital and begged Him to ease Alex's pain.

CHAPTER 21

Amidst all these hospital stays, Alex had been working on mastering his crawling in therapy so we worked with it at home when we could.

One evening when it was time for Alex's bath, we decided to push him further than before. He could crawl by dragging his legs, pulling them up, moving his hands forward, and repeat, but he would only go short little stretches before he would drop to the floor, exhausted. The bathroom was around the corner from the living room and we all got on our hands and knees. We tried to get enough enthusiasm going to get Alex's adrenaline up so he could make it to the bathroom without help. He could be so stubborn and we had to get his mind off of the difficult task if we wanted him to make it the whole way. We all turned into tigers crawling and growling to the bath. It took about half an hour to crawl the four or five yards to the bathroom. We were hoarse from hollering and growling, but Alex made it! I nearly cried when he finally reached the bathroom. It was just so rewarding, but I also knew that the battle was far from over. Alex had an aversion to being told what to do and he could throw a regular fit trying to get out of doing anything he thought we could do for him.

Good thing God installed a stubborn streak in me too.

Though, I wouldn't have minded if He had added a little more patience in the process. There were days of intense frustration. To strive to be upbeat and enthused when Alex was ready to give up before we had even begun was my greatest challenge. I learned the importance of picking my battles. Some things could wait for Alex to want to do them. But once a battle was started, it needed finishing if at all possible. I think it took at least nine months of working with Alex before he chose to crawl on his own because that was how he wanted to get around. He kind of bunny-hopped for a long time before he learned to crawl one leg at a time. And even after he learned, he preferred to bunny-hop when he was in a hurry.

Alex could move his legs quite well, actually. He just had no stability when in an upright position because a lot of the nerves running from his spine down to his legs were not connected. He was good enough at swinging his legs that he was able to get one into a good enough swing to whack the sister or brother beside him in the face when they annoyed him in the van. He had no control of where his foot landed, but if he managed to whack them, he was happy.

We taught him how to pull himself up onto the couch. It took some experimenting before we figured out the best way for him to do it. He loved doing this because then he could see out the window. That gave him the incentive to work hard at it. But it still took weeks of building up muscle before he could do it on his own. Most of what Alex did took upper-body muscle with little to no help from his lower body. He had no feeling in his feet and no muscle tone so he wore braces to prevent drop foot from setting in and to protect his feet from getting injured. One day, Lissandra asked him if he could wiggle his toes. She showed him how she could wiggle hers. He was undaunted by her request. He simply reached down, picked up his foot and manually wiggled his toes. That would teach his smart sister. He could wiggle his toes, too!

The time came to teach him to dress himself. This was challenging and he actually was rather excited about it ... for a while. Then it became a chore and my patience was sorely tested. What Alex couldn't do that other kids did — like run through the room, jump on furniture, or climb the shelf and dump the paint — he made up for with his mouth. He could sass and argue for five; never mind the daggerous names he invented for people when he was angry. It was the one thing he could do to make himself feel in control. Some days, I wished it was the paint he had gotten into instead of the stream of frustration coming from his mouth. He fought dressing himself for nearly a year even though he could do it very well himself. He thought I could do it for him. In fact, he let me know that I was really quite mean to make him do it. It was a duel every morning. But every now and then he would surprise me and not complain. I even tried incentives like a sticker chart. It worked great for about four days before he would get discouraged and be uncooperative, so no sticker. Then he would get upset because of that. He had such a hard time understanding cause and effect, and "consequences for your actions" was a completely Greek to him.

He was able to move his feet to walk, but it took months of therapy before he could even begin to budge his walker on his own. Because his hip was subluxed (not completely in the socket because of so little muscle tone) it made his left leg longer than the right, so he had to have a half inch lift put on his right shoe.

He hated to walk. He tired quickly and I never knew for sure how far to push him. I knew that some kids with spina bifida are often not very motivated. You have to push to get them to do things. With that in mind, I pushed. Alex resisted. I tried to make it fun, but he seldom thought it was worth the trouble. He enjoyed it the most when he could kick a ball while walking. This was very tedious for mom, but helped to make the walk more worthwhile. Some days it took every ounce of strength and willpower for Alex to move a few feet across the floor.

I hope this all hasn't sounded all negative because it wasn't. The harder you work for something, the more you appreciate it. But I cannot just say it was a bed of roses either. Every child has their challenges to face. That's why God gave them parents: to help them through them. Or that's why God gave parents children ... to teach parents how to parent?

One thing it did for us was give life a special purpose even though sometimes we weren't exactly excited about our set of challenges. But then, if we got to choose our challenges, would we be any happier?

I had one more challenge that was probably the hardest to cope with. Because of Alex's incontinence, he had a dirty diaper more often than not. On a bad day, I would change up to six or seven dirty diapers and on a good day only three out of five would be dirty. And on a really bad day he would have the runs and that meant we went nowhere until it was over. Out came a big towel for Alex to sit on and out came the probiotics. I have a very strong sense of smell, so there was no ignoring the obvious and I was kept hopping some days, keeping Alex smelling good. We often asked Alex if he smelled like roses when we thought we smelled a bad diaper. We tried not to be negative about something he could not control and usually found something to laugh about to help us through not-so-pleasant situations. He was five when we finally had a cecostomy tube put in so he could empty his bowels on the toilet and stay mostly clean in between. That is for a later chapter, though.

Meanwhile Alex had a hernia to get fixed, so we added another surgery to the calendar.

CHAPTER 22

Alex was learning to compensate and find other ways to do things when his legs wouldn't cooperate. He would try to get on a little rocker where he loved to sit and look at books. His legs would get all in the way so he would reach down with his hands and try to get them where he wanted them. Or if his foot would get caught under the couch, he would just lay still and holler, "Foot caught!" until someone would come rescue his foot.

One day we had been with some friends who had a boy Alex's age. When we got home Alex told us, "Scott walk." Then our hearts just ached. At some point, we knew he would surely notice his friends could run and he couldn't. We just wanted it to not be so soon.

We were amazed at how well he could express himself. At a year and a half he said, "Daddy, I wanna see it," and, "My Daddy sit here." He was polite and said his "please and thank yous," until suddenly a stubborn streak hit and he refused to say "thank you." Then after trying our patience for several days, he took up where he left off and gave out thank yous freely again. He even got fancy in his show of gratitude. He borrowed a phrase from a little song we sang and would say, "Thank you for the world so sweet."

And how he loved to sing! Any piece of paper he found served as a song book, and "the Bible tellth me tho" would peal forth. Or "Twinkle, twinkle little star" word for word.

Ah, we were some proud, proud parents, and his humor brought much joy and laughter. One day he told his daddy, "See face?" and pointed to his little rosy cheek.

Daddy said he did.

Alex said,"Kiss it."

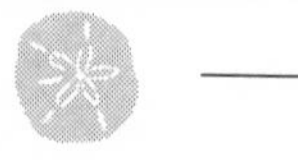

CHAPTER 23

We had had about a two month break with no surgeries. Then in November things just weren't right. We made many trips down to the hospital to get his shunt pressure changed. Alex wasn't too fond of the quick, hard pressure from the magnetic programmer. We tried lowering the pressure and then we tried going up, but nothing seemed to help for very long. So surgery was looking like the only thing left to do. The MRI showed swollen ventricles. Back in we went.

After surgery Alex had a rice-crispy head. We laughed because it felt so funny when we would touch the top of his head. It would crunch just as though we were pressing down on a bag of rice crispies and it would make crackling sound. That happens when air gets trapped in between the skull and the scalp during surgery. It is not painful and eventually works its way out.

We went home as soon as they would possibly let us, but in a few days we were back in with a clogged shunt. Sometimes Alex would get blood clots in his shunt in places that were almost impossible. He was becoming famous for trying everything that wasn't found in the typical handbook.

When family or friends came by to visit at the hospital, it was a special treat. Alex just loved visitors and was ecstatic when his daddy brought his brothers and sister to see him. He also liked the therapy dogs that people brought by to visit. After a dog would do his tricks, Alex would have his stuffed dog do tricks too. It was certainly one of his greatest highlights when a dog full of tricks came by and he would talk about it until his audience (usually Mom) was rather overinformed.

Of course, we got the nurses to disconnect the IV pole as often as we could so we could make our rounds outside. They let us most of the time if we would promise to be back in time for the next dose of meds. And, as always, we went nowhere without people of all ages stopping to talk to us or smile big in passing ... because when Alex smiled it made the world smile.

The nurses adored Alex. They liked Alex's daddy too. Pat loved to bake and whenever he had enough advance warning before a hospital stay, he made brownies for the medical staff on shift. And if we were in the hospital over a special holiday, he would make pies, crisps, and cookies and hand them out. It usually took the help of a Radio Flyer wagon to bring in all the baked goodies.

Once, when we returned from a walk during a stay, we found a poster that said, "Will work for brownies" taped to the wall. No signature, but it didn't take much detective work to find the nurse that was so willing to trade brownies for her services.

And there was a certain doctor that had time in her busy schedule to enjoy some brownie perks too. One April Fool's day we went out on a walk, leaving a pan of brownies in our room much as the three bears had left porridge sitting out. We happened upon said busy doctor on our way back in and she stopped to chat. Somehow in the conversation, she said something about earning brownie points and she laughed like she had told a joke.

We parted ways and getting back to our room decided to eat a snack. We started looking for the brownies, but no brownies were to be found. We asked the nurses if they had seen them. They looked exceedingly innocent — so, so innocent. Then one brave honest soul lowered the facade of innocence long enough to tell us, eyes full of glee, "The person who did it said to tell you if you came asking, 'Happy April Fools!' And here are the leftover brownies."

Then we remembered the brownie point joke that was so funny. Ah! The crazy woman! It was our turn to laugh. Besides being known as "the crazy woman" she was also known as "brownie thief" for a long time after.

We got another little break and went three entire months without any surgeries after that. Alex didn't always feel the best, but we had a peaceful

Christmas at home. We always knew we would go back for more surgeries, but we kept away as long as possible. I guess a gauge for us was that, if Alex had headaches that tylenol or pumping his shunt would cure, we put up with the fussiness. But when he started screaming in pain and nothing helped, we knew it was time for the doctor to take over.

March 5th found us heading for ER again. Alex was admitted and monitored overnight. His regular doctor was on vacation so Dr. M, who was an excellent doctor also, took over Alex's care. He worked very closely with Dr. W. so he was familiar with Alex's complications. On the 6th he did surgery and kept us for a couple days for monitoring.

Twelve days later, I was getting Alex ready for bed and he suddenly started screaming in pain. He had a fever. We knew what that meant. We called Grandpa and Gram to come stay with the children, who were already in bed. We called the on-call Neurosurgery NP and said we were coming down to the ER with Alex and his staff infection. The NP got right on it. She let the doctor in ER know we were coming and to "just do what the Baizes tell you to do. They self diagnose!" We got to the ER at 2:30 am and that's where we were the rest of the night. We were well entertained, though, as the ER doctor was full of fun stories up his sleeve and had plenty of time to chat. In the morning, Dr. W. came in and confirmed our diagnosis. Alex's poor little head had infection in it. She would have to externalize his shunt until the infection was gone.

This began a confusing, difficult time for us. We found out about hospital politics very quickly. We innocently made a comment that started all the trouble. We were talking to Dr. W. about Alex's infection and wondering how he got it. She always spoiled us and had Alex's whole head shaved when she did shunt revisions. Dr. M. didn't. He just shaved around the area he needed to work on. We naively wondered if that had somehow contributed to his infection. It didn't seem as clean to us to have hair so close to the incision. Dr. W. suddenly became vague and soon left.

Alex was on an antibiotic that gave him the hives so they had to switch medications, but we became frustrated as Dr. M. seemed to be taking over Alex's care. We felt slighted and confused. We just couldn't get our dear Dr. W. to come by and take over. We were there for ten days with Alex's shunt draining in a bag beside the bed before Dr. M. put his shunt back in. Alex then developed a swollen abdomen so we stayed another seven days for monitoring. When we finally went home, Alex still was not doing very well. It seemed our every breath was a prayer during that time as we longed for answers. We made several trips down to the clinic to change the settings on Alex's shunt, hoping we would find a perfect setting that would keep the pressure in his head at a comfortable level.

Dr. W. took Alex back after we begged her. It was later that we would find out what had happened. When a patient gets staff infection, the doctor who did the surgery where it originated has to take the case until the problem is taken care of. This protects the other doctors from any lawsuits that might occur. Suing was not part of our vocabulary so that had never entered our minds as being the reason for Dr. W. stepping back. We were glad to have that behind us and have our dear, crazy, fun Dr. W. back.

Alex had a surgery in May and another one in June, trying to find the right size of shunt and shunt assist. But it seemed we were getting nowhere. In July, scans showed Alex had an arachnid cyst between his ventricles. These cysts are non-malignant but can gather fluid and create great discomfort. A burr hole was made in his skull so that a catheter could be inserted. This catheter was like a straw full of holes. It was connected up to his other catheter that was draining the fluid from his ventricles. Of course, his scalp covered this small hole, but if the fluid wasn't draining fast enough we could feel it as it formed a bubble over the hole. The burr hole seemed to help relieve the pressure a little, but Alex was now having neck pains and at times his hands hurt so badly he would wring them and just cry and cry, begging for relief.

Alex's Chiari Malformation was causing him neck pain. Spina bifida causes Chiari Malformation Type 2. It occurs when the cerebellum is not formed properly and it hinders the fluid in the head from circulating through the spinal cord. That in turn causes hydrocephalus, or Water Head. But the

Chiari can cause many problems, as it can tighten up the neck and affect balance. Alex would have to have a Chiari Decompression Surgery which is done by removing a piece off the top of the spinal cord or some of the cranium.

He also would need to have a surgery to detether his spinal cord because it had attached itself to his spine and was tightening up his back. That's what was causing his hands to hurt. These surgeries were set for August.

Lissandra and her class had a reenactment of the Pilgrims and Indians at their first Thanksgiving feast. We were glad it was between surgeries so we could be part of the fun. I had gotten in the habit of buzzing Alex's hair before he went for surgery if at all possible. Knowing he would be soon going for surgery, I gave him a mohawk so he could be an Indian at the play. We called him Chief Scar Head. He looked like a great little warrior which he was indeed!

We also managed to go camping. I would say we all enjoyed it for the most part. It just took some of the fun out of it, seeing Alex not feeling well. But we were by a shallow river and he could sit in the water among the rocks and splash, which he loved doing.

We knew his two upcoming surgeries would be painful and complex so we enjoyed every minute of freedom we could, blissfully ignorant of how complex and painful it really would be.

CHAPTER 24

Tuesday, August 11, 2009 we were at the hospital for Alex to have his decompression done. The surgery went well. He was on heavy pain killers afterwards. There was a button attached to his IV where the pain meds went in. If I thought he was in pain I was supposed to push the button to send a dose of painkillers to him. Well, I thought less is better and Alex was tough. But he was in such pain that he slept twenty-two hours out of the day. I was distraught. They explained to me that if you don't keep up on the meds the pain can get out of control and it is hard to get caught back up. So we pumped in the meds.

He literally slept five days straight. Dr. W. would call me personally before bed and check on how things were going because she didn't trust the nurses to report properly. Or I could call her direct if I felt the nurses weren't understanding the situation, which happened at times. Some nurses were so easy to work with, but some just seemed to miss the point.

Sunday afternoon, we had several friends come see us. It was so good to get out of the room. We tucked Alex away in a wagon with his IV pole trailing along beind and went for a short walk. Alex was still pretty much out of it, but seemed to be staying awake for longer periods of time.

Whenever we went to the hospital, we would wish with all our might that Alex would get a room with windows looking out to the back of the hospital where we could see green lawn and maybe get a view of the river. We sometimes got one that faced the inner court and all you could see was a few trees and the opposite wall of the hospital. Although it was very entertaining if the window washers were at work, it was not our favorite view.

During this long, pain-filled stay at the hospital, we were given the best room in the whole complex. I feel very much that God had a hand in us having this particular room during this time. It was a room on the corner of one of the wings. It was originally intended as a play room, but it never got used for that. It had floor to ceiling windows on two sides. Alex had a perfect view of the helipad. He loved watching the helicopter come and go. I was so thankful he had this bright spot while he was stuck inside most of the time.

Down the hall was a teenager who stayed there almost the whole time we were there. We got to know him and his mom quite well. Actually, I think their stay was a bit longer than Alex's. Alex stayed twenty-four days and I think they were there for thirty.

We had some dear friends who had a son who was battling cancer. They had a small camper they used when they were at the hospital for treatments. They brought their camper down for Pat and the children to stay in as often as they could get away to come see us. It was such a Godsend.

Exactly a week after the decompression surgery, Alex had his cord detethering. This was not supposed to be as painful of a recovery, but he was still in the highest levels of pain. He also had severe edema. He was retaining too much of the fluids they were pumping into him. I was up all night one night, watching him. His CO_2 levels were showing low and the alarms kept going off, so they had him on oxygen all night. I was in tears and the nurse and I kept a close eye on him. Shift change came in the morning and the new nurse decided to change the sensor to make sure we were getting a correct reading.

We hadn't been.

The new sensor showed his oxygen levels were normal! I was too relieved to be upset. I was just so glad he was OK.

Meanwhile, his pain levels were indicating something else was wrong. On Friday, he had surgery to change his shunt assist to see if it relieved him of his head pain. No luck.

On Sunday, Pat and the children were there with us and we were pulling Alex around in the wagon. The nurses told us that they were letting children go out to the helicopter and they could sit in the cockpit with the pilot. We took Alex and he loved it, though he was too scared to sit with the pilot.

Dr. W. ordered a test where they inject dye into the bubble that we used to pump Alex's shunt. They would watch where the dye went on an x-ray machine. If the shunt was working correctly it should have all gone down to his abdomen and would disappear as his body absorbed it. Well, some went into his head and the dye that made its way to his abdomen just pooled up there and stayed. That meant his body was not absorbing all the fluid he was putting out. So, the next thing to do was to externalize the catheter (an EVD: a bag beside the bed where the fluid drains into) so we could see if it would relieve the pressure in his head.

By this time Dr. W was fighting the higher ups in the hospital. She needed permission to do this next surgery, but they were thinking she had maybe done enough surgeries on this case, so they were giving her trouble. She could become a tiger when one of her patients was in need. She would do just about anything for a suffering child.

On Monday afternoon she came to our room and told me she was planning on putting in the EVD in the morning. And very quietly told me that if the hospital staff denied her the use of the Operating Room, she would have to do the surgery right there in the room. I believed her. She had brought the EVD supplies with her and stored them in the cabinet. She meant business. We simply loved her. There was a reason we called her "the crazy lady" (that good kind of crazy).

We were relieved the next morning when they came from surgery to get Alex. It was amazing how much better he felt once the pressure was relieved. His poor little abdomen wasn't trying to figure out what to do with all that fluid and his head pressure became more tolerable.

We thought we had found a temporary solution for that problem. We were rejoicing that Alex was feeling better than he had been ... when he got pseudomonas, a form of urinary tract infection because of the foley catheter they had in. There are only a few antibiotics that can fight this infection. He had a reaction to that antibiotic, so he had to take benedryl before each dose. We were wondering what would go wrong next.

It was impossible to replace his shunt before his infection was gone, so we had to wait it out. On Tuesday, exactly three weeks after the first surgery, he went in for one more. Dr. W. put in a new shunt that drained into his atrium where his blood stream absorbed the fluid instead of draining it into his abdomen.

We went home on Friday. I was worried because Alex just didn't feel well. After all he had been through, I felt insecure taking him home when something seemed to still be amiss. The nurse on duty that day sat me down and got really firm with me and said I was just going to have to trust God to help me care for Alex at home, and that it would be alright. She wasn't my favorite nurse and I was a bit annoyed, but I knew she was right. We said goodbye to all the friends we had made and took one last look at the lovely room we called home for twenty-four days, and headed for home and family.

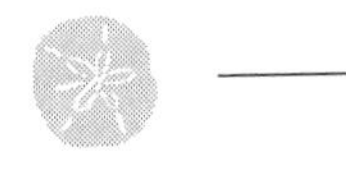

CHAPTER 25

We were off to a rough start. We made trips down to the hospital to change the shunt setting every few days again. Nothing was working.

Dr. W. ordered the dreaded bolt. It's literally a bolt they screwed into Alex's forehead right by his hairline. It had a hole down the middle so a sensor could be inserted into his head to measure the pressure in there. That sensor in turn was connected to a machine that recorded what was going on inside. Very cumbersome and annoying. Alex looked like a little alien with an antenna sticking out of his head. I was to keep a log of his head pressures and record if he felt better sitting up or lying down. They changed his settings on his shunt daily to see if one setting was better than another. All of this was done in Pediatric Intensive Care Unit to try to prevent infection. Going outside was not an option. Thank goodness there was a twelve year old there with a bolt in also. He was so sweet and kindly hung out with Alex as much as possible. It sure made the tedium more bearable.

The bolt was not exactly what one would call worth one's time. Many nurses were skeptical that it helped determine anything. The bottom line was that something was not right and we needed it fixed. The bolt only gave some numbers that may or may not have helped the doctors. We were very relieved on the fourth day to have the bolt taken out and Alex was discharged. We had a month at home. Then, on the 20th of October we went back in to try another size of shunt assist. We were home the next day and on the 27th I took Alex to therapy like usual.

Alex enjoyed going to therapy, but sometimes was less than excited about some of the workouts. He started out fine and then suddenly he just refused to cooperate at all. It was pretty obvious to us that something more than the usual resistance was happening. We decided to end his session early. I got Alex in his car seat and was preparing to back up when Alex grabbed his head and started screaming. Then he started throwing up.

If Alex was throwing up I had a serious problem on my hands. I called Dr. W.'s office and told them I was heading over. I do not know how I did it to this day, other than I had a very active guardian angel at work, plus Alex's angel had to have been busy too; but I let Pat know so he could arrange for the children to be picked up from school for me. And I drove as fast as the heavy traffic and the speed limit would allow.

I don't know how much I actually watched the road. I was constantly checking on Alex. I could reach back and hold his hand as he cried in pain. Then I could relax a bit as he would suddenly fall asleep. Sleeping was not a good thing when he had so much pressure in his head, but I was glad for the break. I had hurried him down to the hospital many times, but he had never been in such pain that he threw up or couldn't stay awake. I wished many times that Pat was with us! Alex would jerk awake and cry in pain and then I would hold the "puke bucket" (we always carried the little ice water pitcher with us that they give at the hospital for Alex to puke in) while trying to drive with one hand until I could pull over beside the road. I think I pulled over three or four times in that forty minute ride. I was beyond concerned! Alex rarely threw up, even when his head really hurt.

I ran Alex into the neurosurgery clinic. They were waiting for me. They were concerned, but became even more so when they took his temperature. It is not uncommon for people with hydrocephalus to have their temperature drop instead of go up when they get very sick. Alex's was around ninety-four degrees. They got warm blankets to try to warm him up and raise his temperature.

They sent me to get a CAT scan of his head and heart done so they could get an idea of what was going on. I put Alex in a wagon and raced through the halls. We had to wait in a crowded waiting room. Alex kept crying, sleeping, and throwing up in turns. People stared. No one likes it when others expose their children to a contagious flu. They had no idea this was not a flu. It felt like glares were coming from some.

CAT scans don't show as much as we need to see, sometimes. Often, the doctor just has to go in and find out what is wrong. As soon as Dr. W. read the results, she called for emergency surgery. I don't know if the scan told her anything or not. Alex was very sick and she was on her way to fix it!

It seemed like a very long time before she came out of surgery to talk to me. Alex was doing fine. Surgery had gone well. She had found a blood clot at the end of the catheter that went into his atrium. It was not unheard of, but neither was it something she saw a lot. Alex seemed bent on trying the less traveled paths.

On the 29th, something went wrong again. I was so glad we were still at the hospital. This time the shunt itself plugged up. It felt like emergencies had become way too normal. We went home on the 31st, ready to get back to normal life again. To our great joy, we were as normal as could be for the whole month of November. We even got to be home and have family over for Thanksgiving Day!

We were just getting all comfortable without any more emergency runs when Alex did it again! I had put the children to bed and was rocking him. He was not settling down and seemed uncomfortable. He suddenly screamed in pain and we knew we would be driving to the hospital yet that night.

Pat called his mom and dad and asked them to come spend the night at our house so the children could just stay sleeping. They came right away. I was so, so thankful for their help.

We packed up and headed out. This was getting too familiar. What was worse was what Dr. W. found. A blood-clot in an unheard-of place. There is the catheter going from the ventricles to the shunt. Then there is a shunt assist that helps control how much fluid goes out. From there, the catheter continues down to the heart. There is a one way valve in there so nothing can go back up into the shunt, but Alex managed to defy the system and got a blood clot up in the shunt assist. It had to have gone up the wrong way past all the "Do not enter!" signs. There just isn't much security a parent can get from that kind of thing.

Alex did better again after surgery and he had a free flowing shunt again. Dr. W. was not sure why he kept getting clots. There didn't seem to be any easy answers to this mystery, and you can't relax when there are so many "not supposed to happens" happening. We hoped and prayed the rest of Alex's life wouldn't be a series of constant emergencies.

CHAPTER 26

To our joy, all blood clots and shunt plugs went on a long lovely four month vacation. We enjoyed the break immensely, but it wasn't a time where we thought we were out of the woods. Alex was at a Level 4, if we were to rate how he felt; 10 being the worst and 1 being the best. It wasn't the quality of life any parent would want for their child. We just wanted to believe there had to be something better.

On April 9th we went in again to change the size of the shunt. It seemed we had tried every size and shape of the great programmable shunt that worked like a charm for 98% of the children. We went home knowing we were at a dead end. We prayed with a greater intensity that God would supply us with answers.

I began doing shunt research online. I read up on all the different kinds. It looked like mass confusion to me. What worked for who? What would work for Alex? I kept looking. The answer or clue had to be there somewhere! I remembered God's promise to us before we got Alex, that we could bring our child to Jesus for answers just like mothers had done so long ago. Then I found an article that caught my attention.

A man wrote how he had tried every shunt there was over a period of eighteen years. Nothing worked for him. Not one to give up, he kept looking and trying. At last he found a shunt that worked differently than all the others. It was a simple, non-programmable shunt called the OSVII.

Pat and I talked it over. Maybe Alex would do better with that style of shunt. We became more and more convinced it was worth a try. We were tired of seeing Alex suffer and tired of trying every setting on his shunt just to see no lasting results.

After two months of no surgery, but constant hospital visits for setting changes we decided to sit down with the doctor and share our plan. To our grief, Dr. W. was on vacation. We would need to see Dr. M.

I sat down with Dr. M. and told him what I had found in my research. Would he consider trying this OSVII shunt? What was another surgery? If it failed we would have at least tried a different dead-end road than the one we were stuck on.

I was really nervous asking him. He was a very intelligent man. He knew a whole lot more about shunts than my brain would ever know. He had even invented the shunt assist! And I was asking him to put in a shunt that didn't need his little invention that helped so many people. I felt like a little ant asking the big bear, could he please use that other path instead of the one he used every day so he wouldn't squish my baby ant?

The big, serious, scary bear said he would honor my request! But he obviously could promise nothing. If it failed we would have to go back to what we had been doing.

Prayer is such a comforting thing when life is so incomprehensible. At the other end of that prayer is a great God with beautiful answers and promises that never fail.

They told us that with this new shunt, every five years Alex would need to have the catheter to his heart replaced until he quit growing. Five years sounded like a nice long vacation to us. We would take that risk.

Dr. W. got back in time to put in the new shunt. Everything seemed to be going well after surgery. We left with high hopes. We stopped for lunch before we went on to visit Nathan and Frances, who were back from Tanzania.

Alex started throwing up after lunch. Our high hopes took a dive to the lowest lows. We called Dr. W. We wondered if we should go right back to the hospital. The odd thing was that Alex didn't really seem to be in much pain, if any. She told us to just keep an eye on him. She didn't think it was shunt related.

With much trepidation we drove away and thus began a new lease on life for Alex. The change was amazing! Even though he would suffer from headaches at times, it was easily resolved with tylenol or we would use the little bulb by his shunt to pump out extra fluid when the pressure got too high. He began throwing up over the smallest things. Certain foods that are harder to break down, like cabbage or eggs or something a bit too greasy, would set him off. The puke bucket was at its post at every meal and in every car ride.

We puzzled over this for years. Doctors could not explain the mystery and all testing came back clear, until Alex's primary care doctor (NP) in Arizona explained to us what he thought had happened. Alex had had so much pressure on the part of the brain that tells you to throw up when he really needed to, that it had actually not been able to send the signal like it should. When the new shunt was put in, it relieved all that pressure and then that signal worked overtime. After a few years, this problem slowly diminished and his little puke bucket no longer followed him everywhere.

And to our joy, at year five, a CAT scan showed the catheter to be plenty long and didn't need to be replaced. It stretched to ten years, and an MRI again showed no shunt surgery was needed.

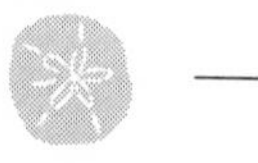

CHAPTER 27

We moved to Arizona a few months after the new shunt was put in. We were sad to leave the familiar hospital and doctors behind. We were enjoying the freedom the new shunt gave us, but it did feel a bit scary to go to a new place and have to learn to know and trust a whole new team of doctors. We knew Jesus would guide us in Arizona like he had in California and our adventurous spirit kicked in as we started a new chapter in our lives.

Alex was three when we moved and he missed his home in California, but he soon learned to love our rented home in Arizona. The house had low windows in every room so Alex could crawl up to them and watch the outside world. The yard was definitely not Alex-friendly. There was no grass to play in, only rocky ground. There was a not-so-gentle drop off just a few yards from the house down to a small wash. Some of our good friends had pooled their money together and bought a toddler-sized four-wheeler for Alex and modified it so it had hand controls. He would go around and around the yard as long as the battery held its charge. I was always nervous about him falling down the steep hillside. Twice my fears were realized. One time was because he had some little friends over and they were helping push Alex around after the battery had gone dead. In their helpfulness, they got too close to the edge and over he went. By some miracle he only got a few scratches.

We became restaurant owners and much of Alex's days were spent at the restaurant. People were always charmed to see a cute little black haired guy in an itty bitty wheelchair and would stop to talk to him. When they asked him direct questions about himself, such as what his name was, he would hang his head in paralyzing shyness and look for mom or dad to answer for him. They were sure he couldn't talk at all. But if he was looking at a book or magazine and someone would sit down beside him and start asking him about the pictures... Ah, then he would talk. He slowly formed friendships with customers. They would invite him to sit with them at their table and they would have a good old chat together. He always got excited when customers would slip him some spending money. He would find one of us to show us his treasure. If he wasn't there, people would miss him and ask where he was. They were in awe at how such a little guy could get around by himself in a wheelchair.

Alex began having stronger headaches and we grew concerned. We saw his new neurosurgeon, Dr.

B., and all testing showed things were running as they should. She asked if there were any changes in Alex's life that could be triggering the headaches. That's when we realized he was getting his molars in and Dr. B. said she was sure that was the cause of his headaches. What a relief!

We were two hours from Phoenix Children's Hospital and from CRS (Children's Rehabilitative Services) where Alex went for spina bifida clinic every year. We had a great team at CRS but had a bit of a frustrating time with the dietitian who was always very concerned that Alex was not gaining enough weight. He was a healthy child with a good complexion who seldom got sick, and we simply were not as concerned as she was. This seemed to concern her even more.

Because Alex has a neurogenic bowel it became necessary to have a cecostomy tube put in. It is a plastic tube that looks like a curly pig's tail connected to a rectangular button with a little lid. They put the curly pig tail part in through a tiny hole in his abdomen on the right side and it ends in his large bowel. Only the button is on the outside, snug against his skin. We had tried other methods to help empty his bowels out and they simply did not work. He had such severe cramping, hand pain, and throwing up when we tried that we knew it was not going to work without the cecostomy tube.

The purpose of this tube is to run a water solution through it and clean out his bowels. This in turn was supposed to keep him from having dirty diapers. I was truly excited about no more dirty diapers. We were told to flush him out once a day. They told us that for most people it took forty-five minutes at first and then usually could be done in half an hour. That sounded great to us, although I was not anxious to begin a new routine. Alex had the procedure done at the Children's Hospital and we stayed there overnight.

I was so nervous about getting the solution right and hooking everything up without pulling the little pig tail tube out. If it was pulled out, we had to insert a special tube they gave us so the hole wouldn't close up and get him to ER as quickly as we could. That scared me silly.

We decided to call his emptying out trips to the bathroom "feeding the pig." It would be our secret code. We bravely got Alex all settled on the toilet, got our potion mixed, and poured it into the GI feeding bag (hanging from the shower curtain rod) that connected to his pig tail tube. I had to learn how to adjust the flow of solution going through his bowels. Too fast caused cramping and too slow didn't get the job done. It was trial and error until we had the perfect solution and perfect flow to get Alex emptied out. But where was perfect? I wasn't exactly enjoying my pig chores.

It didn't take more than a few minutes for Alex to be in complete agony. His cramping was awful. I slowed the flow down to a drip. He threw up more than once. He was on the toilet for two hours before I finally got him off. He was not empty as we soon found out. He had sat in pure misery for two hours of cramping and getting his stomach massaged in a circular motion. I felt so bad. The next day wasn't any better so I called the nurse. She suggested different things to try. It took weeks before we found a somewhat successful pig feeding. Alex again proved that what worked great for others was not what worked for him. We managed to shorten his time on the toilet to an hour and forty-five minutes on a good day. We read stacks of books in between the screams and cries of agony. We had to use double the recommended amount of solution. My hand would ache from massaging his poor little tummy every few minutes.

Throughout the years we managed to shorten the time down to one and a half hours. His cramping was much less and he didn't throw up as easily once we learned that he needed to wait three to four hours after eating to feed the pig. We also found out it worked great for Alex to not empty out every day. We stretched it to every other day and then to every three days. That gave him a break in between his long bathroom stops. Even with skipping days he still had a clean diaper. Later he graduated to pull-ups, though he still had to stay close to home if he had the flu. There was no place like home when he had stomach trouble.

As life is, we slowly learned other methods to help make things easier. We learned that charcoal pills and probiotics had a great way of helping his upset stomach. It certainly was a great thing for stopping the flow for Alex. Sometimes a person wonders why such a simple answer doesn't come sooner. But that is life. We don't get all our solutions and answers at once. We sure were mighty thankful for that little charcoal pill solution when we did get it.

Another answer came when he was eleven years old. We were given the idea of putting his miralax directly into his flushing solution rather than give it by mouth. It worked like a charm. It shortened his toilet time to an hour and fifteen minutes.

Alex had another odd thing that puzzled the doctors and frustrated the insurance company. Cecostomy tubes are normally changed out once a year. It is a five to ten minute procedure to change out the old tube and put in a new one. No anesthesia is given. Alex had to have his changed out every four to eight months. It would get very painful and sore and it would even start breaking by the button. He hated to go in to have it done, but most of all he still could not bear the separation when he went back for the procedure. I always promised I would be right there when he came back. He would often throw up because of his agitation about mom or dad not going in with him. But a new button always relieved the pain and he was glad he had gotten it changed out.

Only once did we have to make a trip to ER because the pig tail got pulled out. Well, it was only part way out. We were getting ready to go on a trip and Alex was on the toilet emptying out that morning. I was running around, washing and packing like a mad woman. I had finally gotten Alex pretty much emptied out and went to disconnect the hose from the the button. I always was very precise and careful doing this so I wouldn't pull the tube out with it. This time, I missed the important step of holding the button firmly against him before I pulled. Alex hollered out in pain and we looked in horror at the pig tail hanging half in, half out. I made a frantic call to the doctor and received calming instructions to just put the usual wound patch over it so it would stay in place and come on down to ER as soon as we could, but that it would be OK.

I was shaking as I loaded Alex up and made the two hour trip to Children's ER. I soon realized our ER experiences at PCH simply were not going to be the smooth ride we had had in California. This was our first round in ER (or ED as it is now called, but I can't make my mind switch to calling it that yet).

We sat in an ER room for a blessed five hours. We saw several doctors and I had to keep Alex from eating or drinking because he was having surgery.

What?! I had to explain several times that he would *not* need surgery. They seemed to have never had to deal with a vagrant pig tail before. It was a simple procedure up in radiology to get the new tube installed. All we needed was to be sent on to radiology. They finally got tired of us taking up a bed and gave Alex a snack and sent us to get the tube replaced. Twenty minutes later, we were all set and heading home. That was five extra hours away from my packing. Add the four hours travel time and twenty minutes actually doing something productive ... that's around nine and a half hours I would somehow have to compensate for.

I was very very careful at disconnect time after that. I made sure Mr. Pig stayed right where he belonged.

CHAPTER 28

Alex was off to kindergarten when he was six. He struggled to retain all the new things he was being presented. We soon realized he needed an unusual amount of repetition to get a new concept to stick. He ended up taking kindergarten again. We just wanted him to start out with a good, solid foundation.

He went to a small private school along with Marcio and Rafael. It worked very well, having his brothers at school to help him go to the bathroom. They also made sure he was included in a lot of the games, pushing him at high speeds in a game of tag or around the bases. He loved these wild rides. Me, I was sure he would end up in a roll over. Thankfully, he survived it all with hardly a scratch, even though he did have a couple spills.

The children at school loved Alex and would sometimes squabble about who got to push him around. Alex needed help getting around on the playground as the school yard wasn't paved and was mostly gravel and grass. Sometimes Alex would be frustrated because his well meaning little friends took him where they wanted to go and not where Alex wanted to go. I asked the teacher if I could talk to his classmates and explain wheelchair etiquette. They were such good, kind hearted kids. I wanted to give them a better way of helping Alex without dampening their generous, helpful spirits. I simply asked them if they would like a classmate to take them by the shoulders and steer them all over, giving them no control of where they went. With big, wondering eyes they looked at me and shook their heads, no. I explained that Alex's wheels were like his legs. They took him where he needed to go. He really was glad for their help with getting him places, but asking him for permission and finding out where he wanted to go would make him feel like he still had control of his "legs." They all agreed that would be a better way.

It didn't take long to realize that Alex would struggle most with math. We found out that is very common for children with spina bifida. His teachers would sometimes feel so bad they hadn't been able to get a new concept through to him. But it wasn't because they weren't teaching him right. It just took endless repetition for Alex to catch a new concept. Sometimes it was a bit disheartening, but together we would try a new approach. Once he got it installed in his brain he did very well with retaining it as long as he had consistent practice.

The multiplication tables were simply not something he was able to commit to memory. We could have drilled him at home, but by the time he got his homework done his brain was so fried and he was too frustrated to take on anything more. He did much better with having a times table available where he could find his answers for his math problems. Slowly, the facts began to stick.

Thankfully, Spelling and Language were not difficult for him. He read very well, though comprehending what he read sometimes was a bit of a challenge. In time, what he read started making more and more sense to him.

CHAPTER 29

As Marcio and Rafael got older and no longer went to school with him, Alex had to become more independent. He did a pretty good job, but definitely preferred to be dependent. We knew we needed to move to a place where he could get around on his own in his wheelchair. The home we rented was not suitable for him anymore and we couldn't make it accessible for his wheelchair because it was a rental. We did a lot of praying, searching for a good place where Alex could have proper accommodations. We found a lovely home out in the country on five acres. It had a porch around the whole house and the floors inside were made of flagstone so he didn't have to try to wheel around on carpet. The bathrooms were small but workable. The boys had their room in the attic so Alex would crawl up the stairs to go to bed. It was good exercise for him. We couldn't have asked for a more perfect place for Alex. We were thankful to God for granting us such a wonderful home where Alex could enjoy his new freedom and go almost anywhere he wanted by himself.

We had a couple cows, some goats, sheep, and dogs. Alex spent a lot of time with the animals, watching them play. He learned to fill their water dishes and that became part of his daily chores.

We got him an Aussiedoodle when he was nine. We had hopes she would be a protector and a companion for Alex when he was outside. Well, she had a good heart but didn't seem to be too dedicated. Of course, we didn't spend time training her for any special service. We named her Shaggs and she was great at running off with our other dog, Sami, if the gate was left open. Her running around resulted in puppies. They were beautiful, good natured dogs. We kept one of the puppies and named her Alaska. She had more of the personality we were looking for and proved to be very gentle and attentive to the children.

We sold our restaurant about a year after we moved to our little ranch. By this time, we had decided it was time to pursue our dream of adopting again. We went through the foster classes and lived through the paperwork. We also managed to live through a huge turnover of social workers. We finally got our foster/adopt license and right away our social worker told us she had a two year old girl that had been in foster care for less than two months whom she thought would fit our family perfectly. She wasn't free for adoption, but our social worker was fairly confident she would be free in the future.

Did we want to take the risk? We talked as a family and our answer was "yes!"

Lilie came to us the week of Easter. She was our Easter Lilie and stole our hearts right away. She soon became our Tiger Lilie as she struggled with adjusting to her new family. She was very aggressive towards me and Alex. She often would scratch my face and rip my glasses off as she screamed in anger. I would just hold her and give her mom time by sitting together on the couch and looking at a book. She was pretty much non-verbal so her frustration level was sky high. She slowly started relaxing and trusting us a bit more. When she wasn't feeling so frightened about life and all the new adjustments, she was a tease and we had so much fun together.
Lilie was absolutely terrified of church. She fought like a hurt tiger the first few weeks we took her, but, boy, when she finally let herself relax and enjoy it, the social butterfly in her came bursting out of its cocoon. She began living for the weekend so she could go to church. She clung to adults and struggled to make friends with other children. If she sensed even the slightest hint of animosity from another child, the tiger in her would rise up and out would come her nails. But when she felt safe she was a loving, endearing child.

She had speech therapy and she began saying more words. It helped so much with communication, but so often she would become frustrated because she could not say the words right. She often would start her words with the last sound she heard. "Bark" came out as "kar," with the "b" sound completely lost in the struggle to say the word.

One day, several months after she had come to us, she was in one of her rages so I picked her up to hold her close. She reached up to grab my glasses and I just looked at her hoping she would let my love reach her. She suddenly stopped and looked me in the eyes for a few moments and her eyes seem to say, "Oh, I do love this person and she loves me! I don't want to hurt her!" She slowly put her hand down and from that moment on she never attacked my face or my glasses ever again.

We figured out that when she was in one of her rages, if we could say something funny and get her to see the funny side of the situation and get her to laugh, then her anger melted away and she would give in and snuggle up close, a completely changed child.

Alex had enjoyed being the youngest for nine years and he didn't give up that position without a struggle. The meek, shy boy he was in public was seriously in hiding at home. He had many stormy moments as he tried to adjust to his new tiger sister. It didn't help that Lilie felt she could take her frustrations out on him and he was well pinched and slapped for months to come. Oh, the adjustment pains were real! He would sometimes scream that he wished she had never come and she had ruined his life. I would have become a millionaire if I could have gotten a dollar for every fight I had to referee.

In spite of the all scratches and blows, they began finding out they actually loved each other. Alex would ask where Lilie was when he got up and she wasn't around. They learned to enjoy each other and play together in between the thunder storms.

One day, while talking to Lilie's social worker I found out Lilie had a half sister (Ariana) living with a relative. We wanted the girls to grow up knowing each other so we began having visits with Ariana and her grandma. She was a year younger than Lilie and they shared the same birth mother. We had told our social workers that if there was a sibling we would want them to be together and would take him or her, but that message got lost in the changeover of social workers.

Ariana was born with a double cleft lip and double cleft palate. Her parents were young and found the demands of taking care of a little tiger and a baby sister who took extra attention very daunting. Ariana had multiple surgeries and had to be fed with a special bottle. She got an infection and had to be taken to the hospital. Her dad had a cleft lip and palate also and caring for her was hard for him because of the memories it brought back. He was adopted when he was fourteen by Jerry and Connie. Connie had two biological children that had the cleft lip and palate and knew very well the challenges he faced.

Connie welcomed Ariana into her home and fostered her after DCS took over Ariana's case. Ariana had lost her will to live and Connie poured her love into her and gave her baby granddaughter a new reason to live. Ariana was almost two when we began having visits. Connie had already had her for a year. Ariana was very attached to her Nana. Lilie had been kept away from Ariana when they had lived together because of Lilie's tiger approach to her relationship with her baby sister. They certainly had not had a chance to bond. They took to each other like true sisters when we began visits: love one minute and hate the next with Lilie being the aggressive, controlling one. They had some serious bonding to do and it wasn't going to happen overnight!

I had understood that Connie was going to adopt Ariana. But when we met the first time, she told me she needed to find a good adoptive home for Ariana because she was seventy years old and wanted her to go to a younger family. It was so hard for her to do. She did not know that we were open to adopting the two girls together, obviously because of the lack of communication on the part of DCS. We soon had a plan in place and we got together often so we could start bonding. Then in December we began slowly transitioning her over to our home.

She was two when she was finally officially transitioned into our family and it was nine months after Lilie had come. I'm not sure who had the most growing pains and adjustments after that. Ariana certainly had a lot to work through. She was not used to sharing her time with another child and she missed her Nana so much. Connie stayed away for the whole month of January so we could take time to bond and after that we had monthly visits.

Ariana was a not a tiger like her sister and never kicked and screamed. She was more like a turtle that would draw up tight under her shell where she would grieve and mope and let no one in. She was, if possible, more stubborn than Lilie. There were days I just wished she would scream it out of her system. She was completely non-verbal and had no way to express what was bothering her except for crying and being cold to us. It was slow progress with getting her to bond with me. Like Lilie, she loved Pat to death, but Mom was the bad guy. It is so hard to see a child suffer so much. I was very frustrated at times with Ariana's tactics at trying to be in control. This is perfectly normal for any child to try to gain control, but I had never met a more persistent little bit of humanity. And it took a long time for her to realize that she could love Nana and Mom at the same time. She often just cried when we had visits because she was so confused about who to love.

She was so confusing at times. If I sang her a song she would be so happy one time and the next time she would cry and be mad at me. In the first few months she would be a happy little girl as we shopped or went to an appointment and would hum happily as we drove home. But the minute she realized we were getting close to home or when we stopped the van in front of our house she would start silently crying and be cold to me. She seemed to have a switch she could switch off and on and we never knew when it would be. She was the only one who could control it and she hung onto the little bit of her life that she could control with all her might. She was not very responsive to her speech therapist either. She seemed to not want to learn, like holding onto her life just as it was would keep her safe. I longed to just take all her pain and wipe it away with one stroke but, alas, that is not an available option in the process of healing!

Ariana had cleft palate surgery in March of 2017 and having time alone, just her and I at the hospital, actually helped us with the bonding and connecting a lot, even though she was terrified of the doctors and nurses. Her surgery was to finish closing up her palate. Her surgeon did a wonderful job. But, as often happens, it opened back up a bit and she got a lot of food up her nose. A violent sneeze would often clear it up, which was definitely not ideal by any means. So, we got a palatal obturator (it looks a lot like a retainer and clips onto her teeth) made for her little mouth to cover the opening and keep food from lodging in her nose. It was tricky to learn how to put it in each day, but we got the hang of it and it was a life saver.

We obviously needed more excitement in our lives, so we decided to travel to Brazil that June to see my family. It took some crazy hoop jumping to get the proper paperwork to take our foster girls out of country and get them passports and visas. Our children were growing up and starting to sprout wings. Sandi was eighteen and was planning on going to Uganda in July to teach my niece's boys for two school terms, so we knew if we wanted to go on this trip to Brazil with all our children along it had to be that June.

It had been twenty years since I had been there last and my heart just drank up all the sights, sounds, tastes, and smells of my childhood like it could never get enough. Our three weeks there were just too short. And, regretfully, too many of mine and Pat's hours were spent in the dentist chair trying to get some work done at a more affordable price.

It was hard to know I wouldn't see my brother, Lucas. His death seemed unreal to me. I had dreamed of the day I could see him when we went back to Brazil. But this was never to be! I was so excited that it worked out to go to the old home place (it was not being lived in) where I spent the first ten years of my life. My children were bewitched and wanted to buy the farm and move in. And I certainly would have loved that, but a farm like that is worth much more than our humble pocket book could afford.

The trip itself was an amazing feat! To get all of Alex's catheters, wheelchair, and his supplies for three weeks along took up a lot of space in various pieces of luggage. We were each allowed two suit-cases and one carry on. We ended up with fifteen pieces of luggage and, thankfully, not one piece was lost. Getting on and off the plane took a bit of genius work. Each adult had to care for one child and

Alex's wheelchair would be left at the door of the plane while he was carried aboard to his seat. We never were assigned seats all together so we were scattered over the plane. I was having some stomach trouble so I was completely miserable on the flights to Brazil. And did I mention I hate to fly? I wished with all my heart I wasn't an adult so I could sit by Pat and be looked after like one of the little kids.

On the way home it was a bit better and I was the most thankful woman on earth when we were at last back on the ground and got in our van and headed home. It was worth it, though! The children loved it and Alex managed to get his wheelchair through most of their doors and never got a UTI. Although, we all managed to get the flu while we were there. But such wonderful memories we made!

CHAPTER 30

It took almost two years after Lilie joined our family for the girls' adoption to take place. I made the girls matching jumpers for this special day. A joyous day it was, even if Alex had a hard time with his emotions. He always had a hard time when emotions got high and would start crying and could hardly stop. Lilie remembered the courtroom and was a little on edge but enjoyed all the extra attention she and Ariana got. Sandi was still in Uganda so she couldn't be there for the special ceremony, but Ariana's Papa and Nana were there. Afterwards we went and had lunch together to celebrate.

There is something so liberating in finalizing an adoption; in knowing our girls would no longer be removed and have to go through more separation trauma. They had come so far and were healing; learning to let go of their fears and learning to love. We were so proud of them and were amazed at their resilience.

Lilie was making progress and becoming more settled, but she still struggled so much with taking her jealousy and frustration out on Ariana and Alex. Ariana often had scratches on her face in different stages of healing. She was not an aggressive child and I seldom saw her hurting Lilie in any way, but she was good at silently doing her thing. Being my silent one by no means meant she was less frustrated. I never knew for sure if she had antagonized Lilie by a look or a movement because by the time I heard the screaming and crying and got to them — Lilie usually was the one that alerted me to an altercation by screaming and claiming Ariana had hurt her — Ariana looked very innocent and even covered for Lilie and said she hadn't hurt her. But Ariana's face would have big red scratch marks I knew she hadn't put there herself, while Lilie had nary a scratch in sight.

In spite of the rough times, the girls did everything together. Although, there were days that Ariana would quietly play inside while Lilie spent her day in her beloved outdoors. She would try to convince Ariana to come out and often would use force, but when Ariana wanted her space she stood her ground.

Alex was always gentle with Ariana and always stood up for her. But Lilie rubbed him the wrong way and he would become so angry with her. Many times he would try to interfere or mete out what he thought were her just deserts when she became aggressive to him. It was brawl city some days.

Despite the open expressions of frustration and anger, they were learning to love each other. Alex, in true boy fashion, did not stoop so low as to admit he missed them when they were apart, but the telltale signs were there. Many times, Lilie's witty comments had Alex shaking with laughter.

We were so thankful for the support and help we got from our friends and church group we were part of at that time. They were supportive and embraced our children. Alex was loved and appreciated at school. Sadly, not too long later we had a disagreement with this group on their beliefs. One of them being that they were the only True Church of God. We knew God was asking us to let Him be the judge on who was part of His church and could not continue holding ourselves apart from fellow believers who did not have membership with this group.

Our lives changed a lot after we were no longer accepted in their group. It was hard to see the children mourn the loss of their friends. Alex, being an introvert, did not make friends easily or quickly. His loneliness was intense and he went through some very low times. He was able to talk to me about his grief and how much he missed his friends. I was so thankful he could do this, although sometimes it didn't come easily and he definitely needed encouragement to put what he was feeling into words. To add to his list of sorrows, Marcio moved to southern Arizona at age 18, to work for a farmer. Alex missed him so much it about broke my heart to watch his anguish. He was so happy when he turned thirteen and we gave him a phone, so he could keep better track of his bathroom schedule and could communicate with his friends. He began talking with Marcio often and we could see his depression lifting. That brother bond was deep and it was beautiful to see the sparkle come back into Alex's eyes. Though these changes were hard for all of us, we thank God for where He has led us. Our children are blossoming and have made many new friends. And one more wonderful thing that happened was that his big sister Sandi got home from her mission trip that spring.

One of my friends from my former church group did respite for Alex. We were thankful she continued this service after we left their group. Her son is a couple years older than Alex and they are very good friends. Alex loves hanging out with his long time buddy. He also enjoys off-roading with Rafael or tagging along when Rafael goes on outings with his friends. This helps Alex to get out of the house and gives him a chance to make new friends.

Alex has participated in some great programs over the years. When he was six or so, he began horse riding therapy at Horses with Heart. He got to ride one hour a week for six weeks in the spring and again in the fall. This is something he loves very much. He is great pals with the horse he rides and they are always so happy to see each other. For several years now, he has been going to Bartlett Lake Marina (fully handicap accessible) for Arizona

Adadpive Water Sports day. He gets to water ski on skis that have a seat for those that aren't able to stand. He gets to ride the jet ski, go tubing, fishing and kayaking. Another amazing thing he gets to do is go to Camp Patrick in the summer. It is a camp for kids with spina bifida. He can even take a sibling along. These programs were founded by wonderful people who volunteer hours of their time each year to make so many kids smile and experience things they wouldn't be able to otherwise. I pray God's rich blessings on these selfless benefactors who give Alex and other kids so many reasons to smile!

I began homeschooling the kids when Alex was twelve. It was a bit of an adjustment, but he settled into his routine and enjoyed the relaxed way of learning. It took me a bit to adjust to teaching my own kids. Teaching other people's kids sure is less stressful than teaching your own. But with much gracious help from my heavenly Father, I am able to be teacher/mom and have come to enjoy it.

This year Alex entered his teens ... need I say more? We have new challenges to work through; some being quite different than the challenges we faced with our more mobile kids. Alex learned to mow the lawn with the mower we got with hand controls. It was fun at first, but the good old teen attitude of, "Why do I have to do it?" shows up now and then and likes to hang around. The lawn does get mowed, though, in spite of his lack of enthusiasm.

Getting a phone also brought responsibility for Alex. He has alarms set to get himself up in the morning and to help him keep his bathroom schedule on his own. Boy, does it make mom's life easier! And let's say the phone doesn't get argued with as much as Mom does.

But the truth is that my babies are growing up. The girls are cheerful little helpers and have let themselves learn how to love and be loved. They have found happiness and contentment in being part of this wild, crazy family. God has blessed us all so far beyond what we deserve. He has given us so much to find joy in and be thankful for. We never dream for one minute that we could have come this far without His constant presence, healing, and guidance. Daily, He is patiently teaching us to be more like him.

That fall after the girls' adoption, I decided that it was time to clean house of everything baby. We found a new home for the crib and the baby/toddler clothes that were outgrown. I was ready to live life with my six beautiful children and husband of twenty-plus years. You know, just sit back and enjoy the ride.

My ride was short lived. A month later, at forty-one years old, I came down with a serious case of baby fever.

My family was used to me having crazy, hairbrained ideas, but I knew that getting them to see my fever would be an epic ride. I threw out hints to get them used to the idea, but before anyone could take me seriously, a new issue presented itself to me. The baby I dreamed to adopt would be blessed with

Down syndrome. I prayed earnestly about this dream that kept a strong hold on my heart. I couldn't shake it. I tried. I was not mentally ready for all the paperwork once again and the new adjustments that came with the dream. My heart simply would not be silenced. So, I began with a candid talk with Pat. That didn't go so well, but I begged him to pray about it. I think he did, but I think it was more of a "This is how it needs to be, God," kind of prayer. Not a "What do you say about this, God?" Pat finally did say that I could ask the children, but that they needed to have a say in this, too.

I put on all my armor and presented my heart problem to my family. They had to be scraped off the ceiling, but stopped voicing their fine opinions that we were "too old for this" and "Mom has enough to do" long enough to agree to pray about it. I told them that God had given our family a talent — a special love for people that needed a little extra help through life — and hiding our talent in the sand didn't seem like the right thing to do. But I was willing for them to come back with a "no" as long as they got that direction from God and not their own personal desires. So, we all prayed ... and slowly the answers came back. No one could say no when they took their own selfish desires out of the way. It wasn't a blazing green "yes" by any means, but at least it was an OK to work in that direction and leave the outcome up to God.

The three youngest, or the "littles" as we fondly call them, are very excited about a baby brother or sister. And it seems the "bigs" have caught the fever, too. We can hardly wait for that little bundle to arrive.

Of course, Marcio could be exempt from that claim. His attention is quite taken up with his sweet bride Lori, and we are just delighted with the new addition he has brought to our family.

We have challenges ahead we will face. Many are unforeseen, of course. Others we have known we would face sooner or later. One of these foreseen challenges is surgery for Alex. His scoliosis has slowly gotten worse in spite of the upper body brace he wears every day. His ribs are beginning to be affected because of this and it is also causing him some hip pain. He is seeing a spine specialist and will be looking at corrective surgery sooner than we had thought.

Another challenge will be orthodontic work on Ariana's mouth and another surgery on her palate. Thankfully, her procedures will not be for a year or two yet.

So, this is where I will draw the curtain on this tale of our lives. We have so many more beautiful moments we are anticipating God will paint on the canvas of our life story. And maybe we will meet again on the pages of another book sometime in the future, when more strokes on our life story have been added. We look forward to continue working with National Down Syndrome Adoption Network and await the day we have our sweet baby placed in our arms. Just as every other child God has given to us was a part of His beautiful plan, we know we will inevitably say again:

"It was meant to be!"

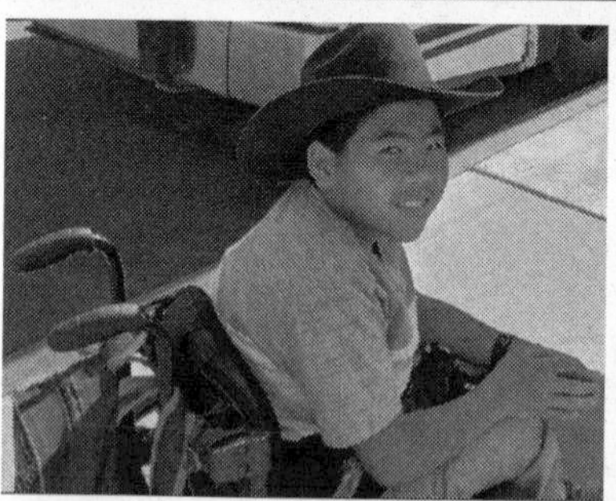

Top Left to Right:

Back: Pat, Sandi, Lilie, myself, and Rafael, Front: Alex and Ariana, fall of 2020. | Alex on his way to Camp Patrick for a week of fun. | My crazy beautiful kids. | Alex (age 3) wearing his beloved little hat after yet another surgery.

Top Left to Right: *Alex a few days old (2007). | Alex enjoying some water skiing at Arizona Adaptive Water Sports Day. | Ariana and Lilie. Best friends. | Alex around the time he stole our hearts. | Ariana's and Lilie's first Christmas with us. | Alex and his beloved therapy riding horse loving on each other.*

SYLVIA BAIZE

Sylvia lives with her husband Patrick and their family at their country home in Arizona. She is a stay-at-home mom and homeschools their three youngest children. She loves the busyness of caring for her family. She also enjoys writing, usually in the quiet of the night while everyone is asleep.